Stars when you shine
You know how I feel
Scent of the pine
You know how I feel
Oh, freedom is mine
And I know how I feel

It's a new dawn
It's a new day
It's a new life
For me
And I'm feeling good

—Leslie Bricusse and Anthony Newley,
lyrics from "Feeling Good,"
as sung by Nina Simone

Lee Friedlander

Prayer Pilgrimage for Freedom

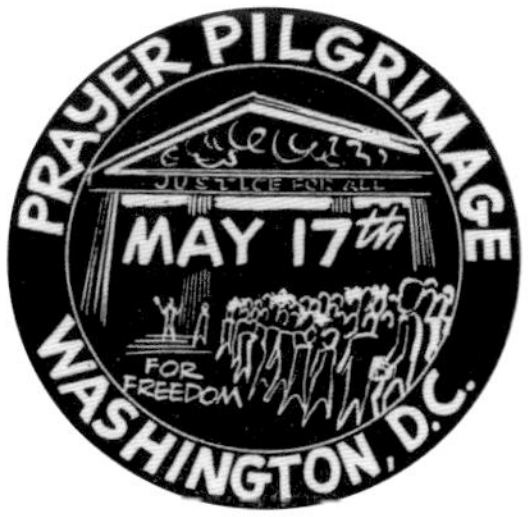

1957

EAKINS PRESS FOUNDATION

The Eakins Press Foundation wishes to thank the National Association for the Advancement of Colored People for authorizing the use of the Program for the Prayer Pilgrimage for Freedom, 1957; source: The A. Philip Randolph papers, and the NAACP papers, at the Library of Congress, Manuscript Division.

ISBN 978-0-87130-071-3

www.eakinspress.com

The publisher gratefully acknowledges support from Furthermore, a program of the J.M. Kaplan Fund.

Furthermore:
a program of the J.M. Kaplan Fund

FOR BAYARD RUSTIN

As the Founding Americans prayed for strength and wisdom in the wilderness of a new land, as the slaves and their descendants prayed for emancipation and human dignity, as men of every color and clime in time of crisis have sought Divine guidance, so we now, in these troubled and momentous years, call upon all who love justice and dignity and liberty, who love their country, and who love mankind, to join in a Prayer Pilgrimage to Washington on May 17, 1957, where we shall renew our strength, communicate our unity, and rededicate our efforts, firmly but peaceably, to the attainment of freedom.

A. PHILIP RANDOLPH **REV. MARTIN LUTHER KING, JR.** **ROY WILKINS**

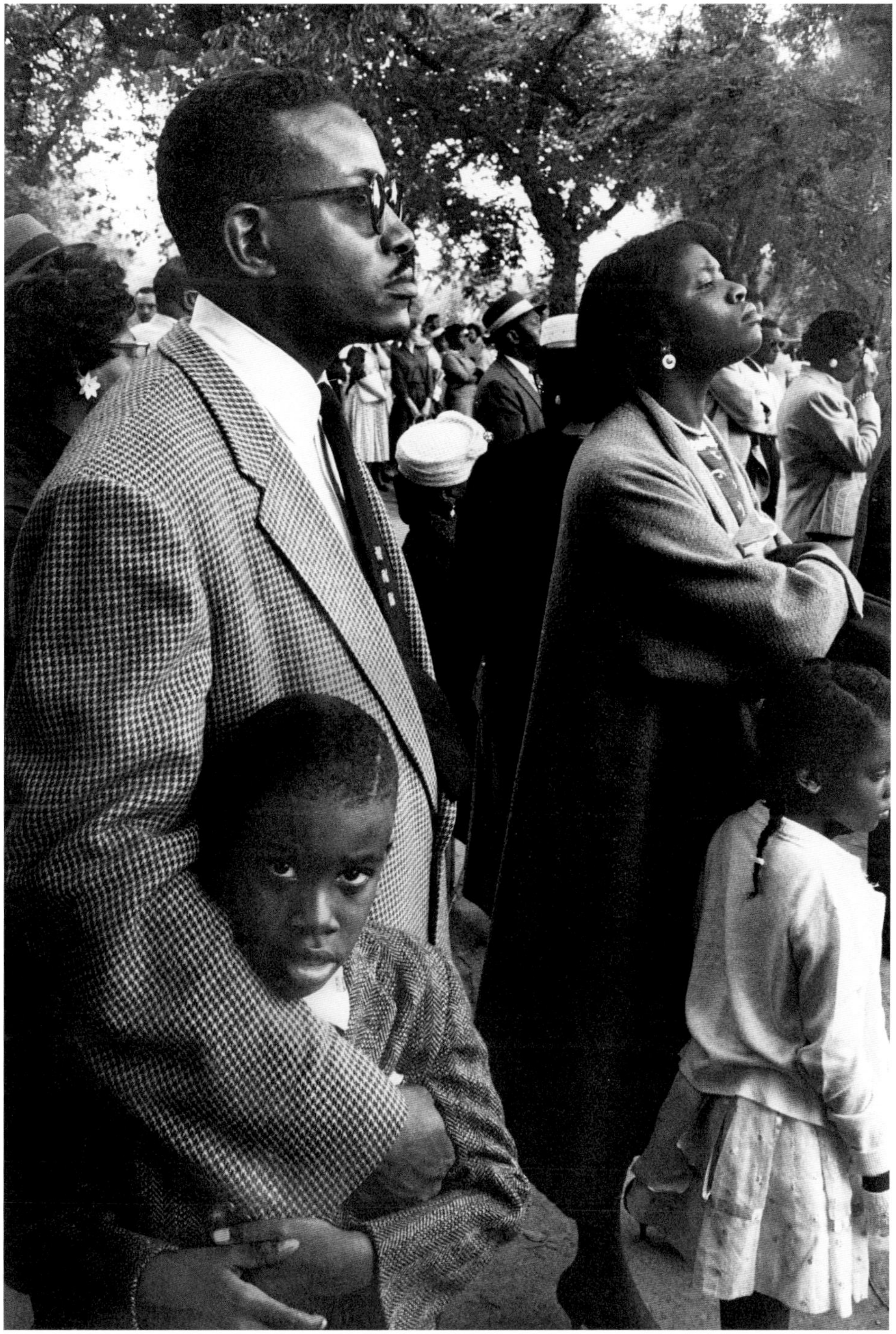

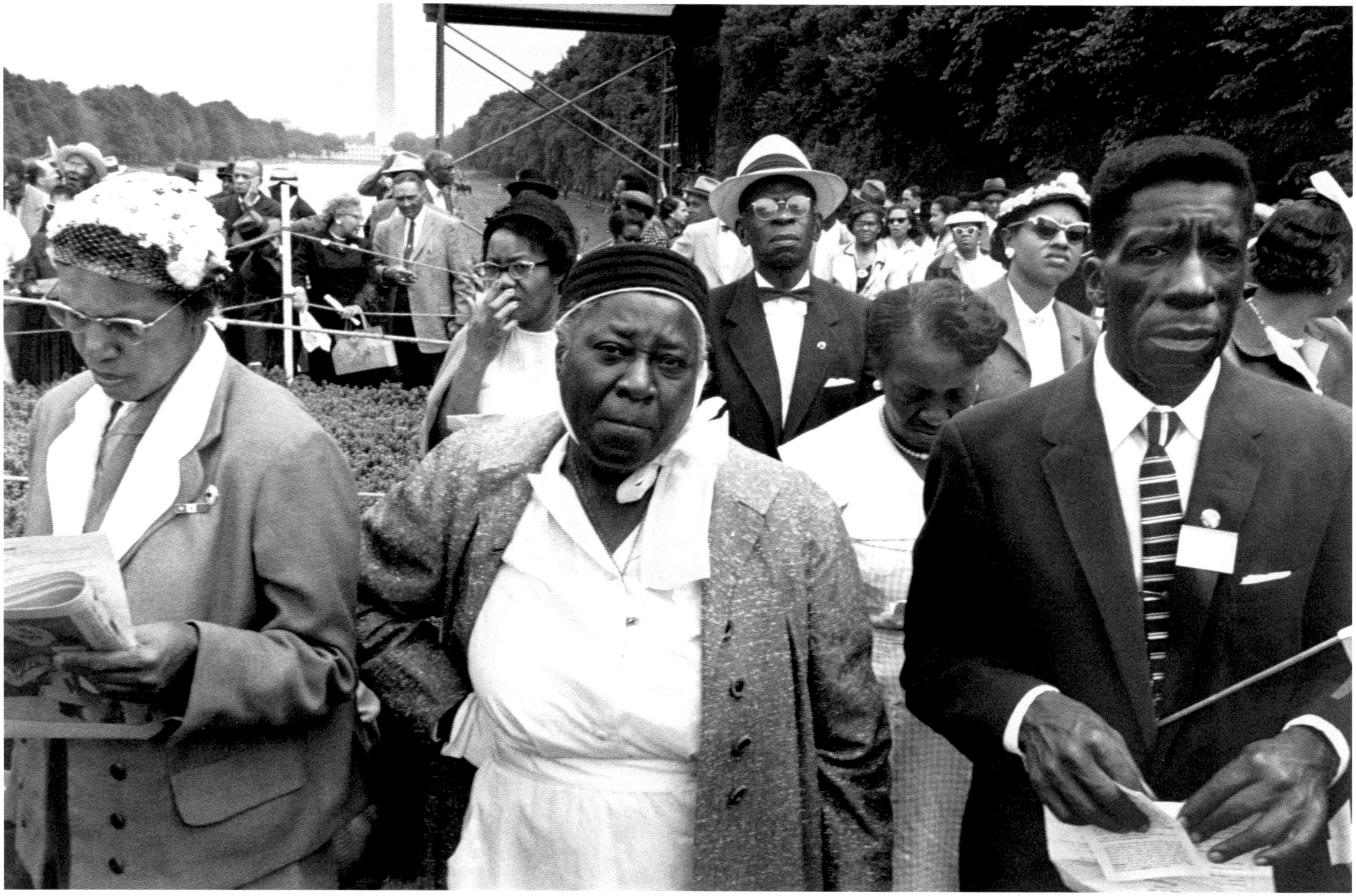

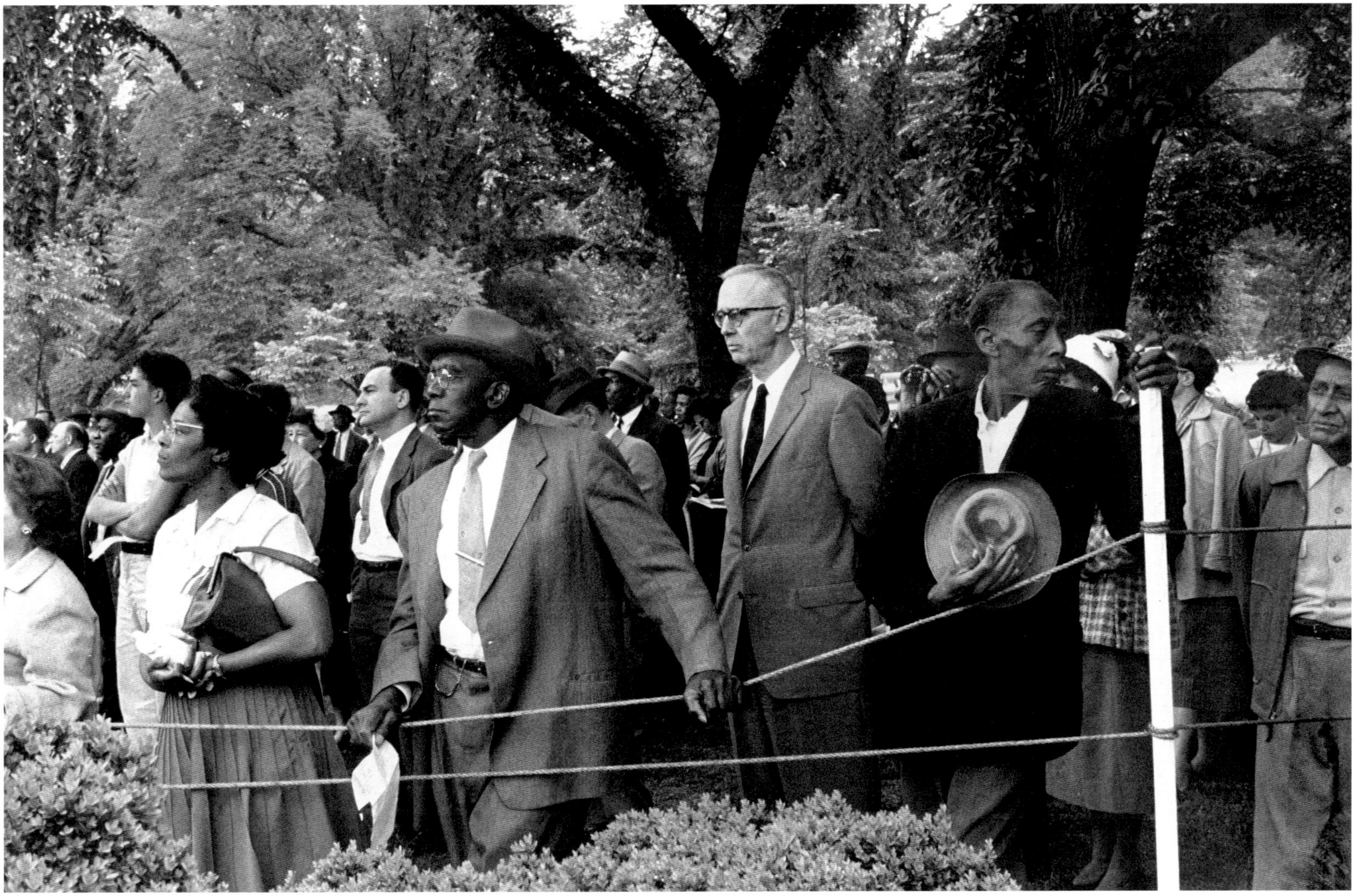

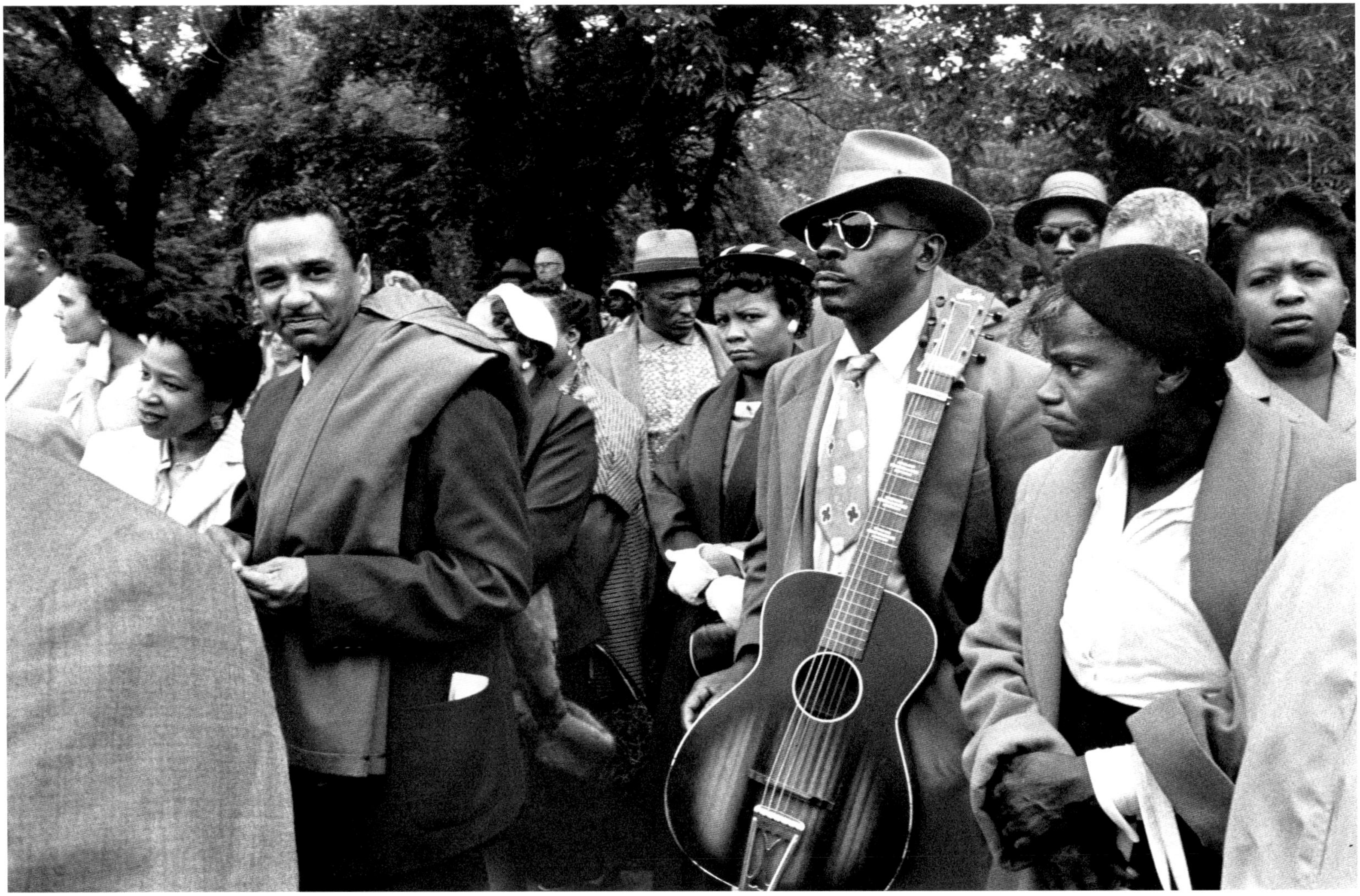

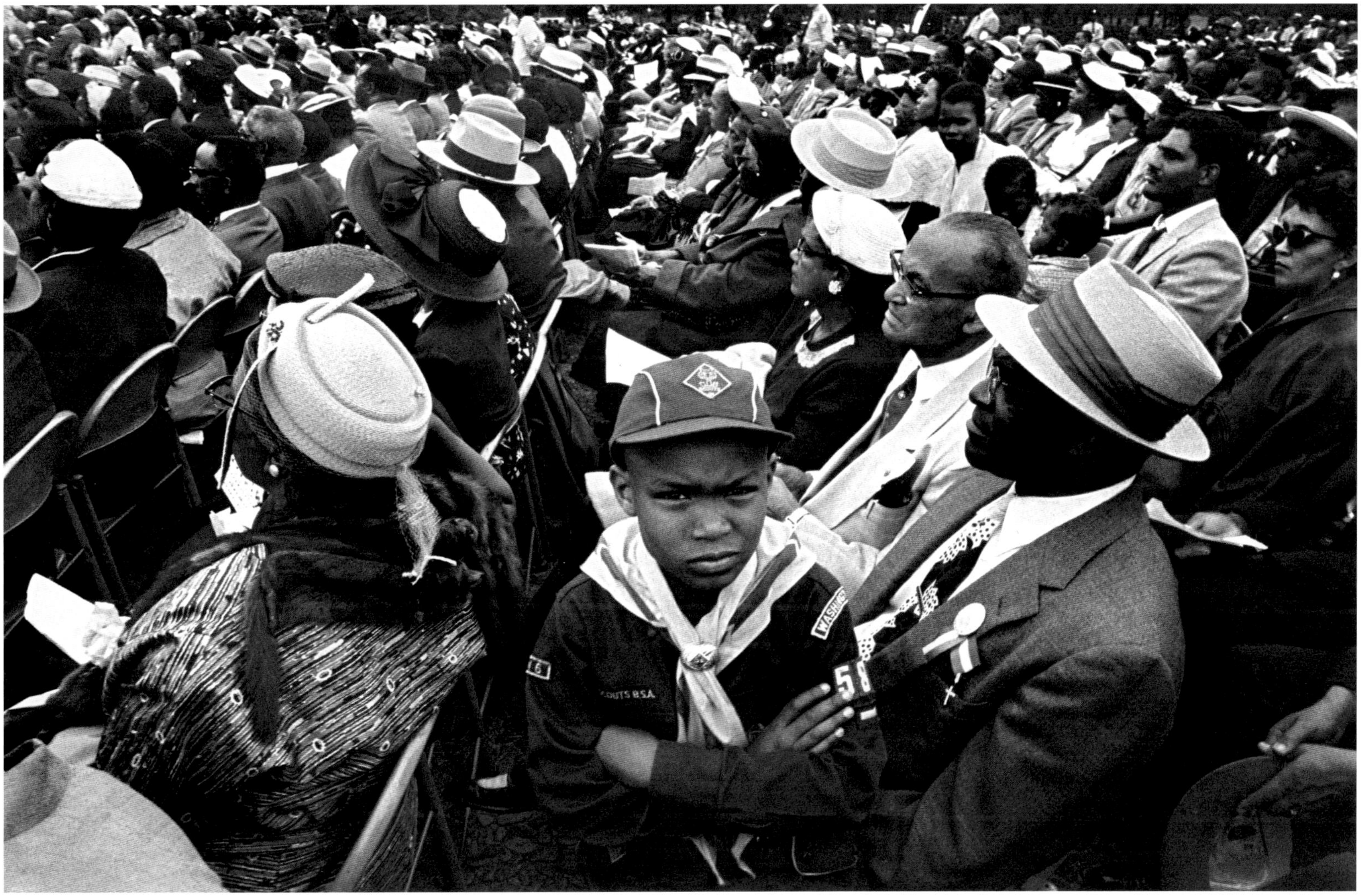
16
58

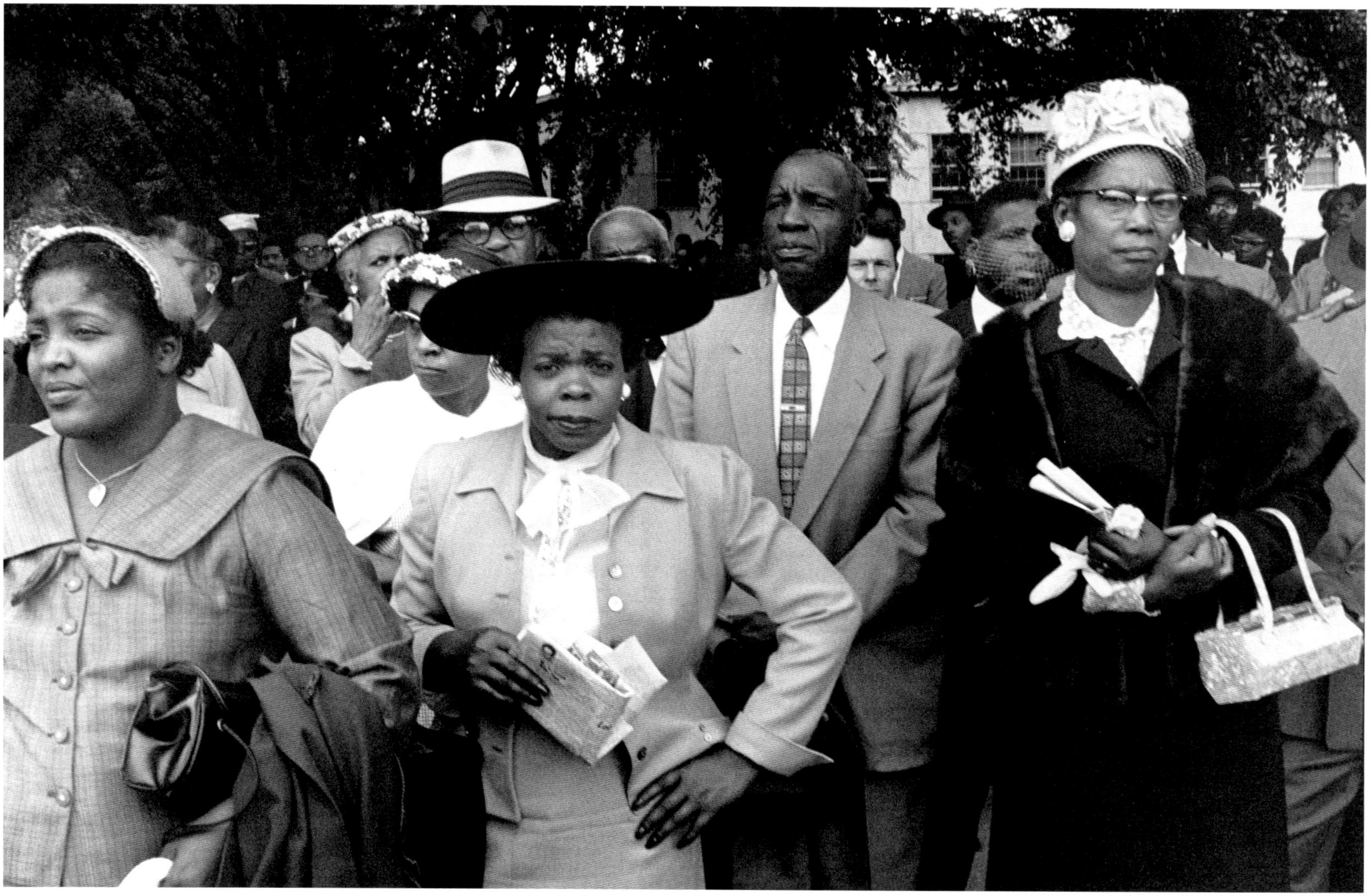

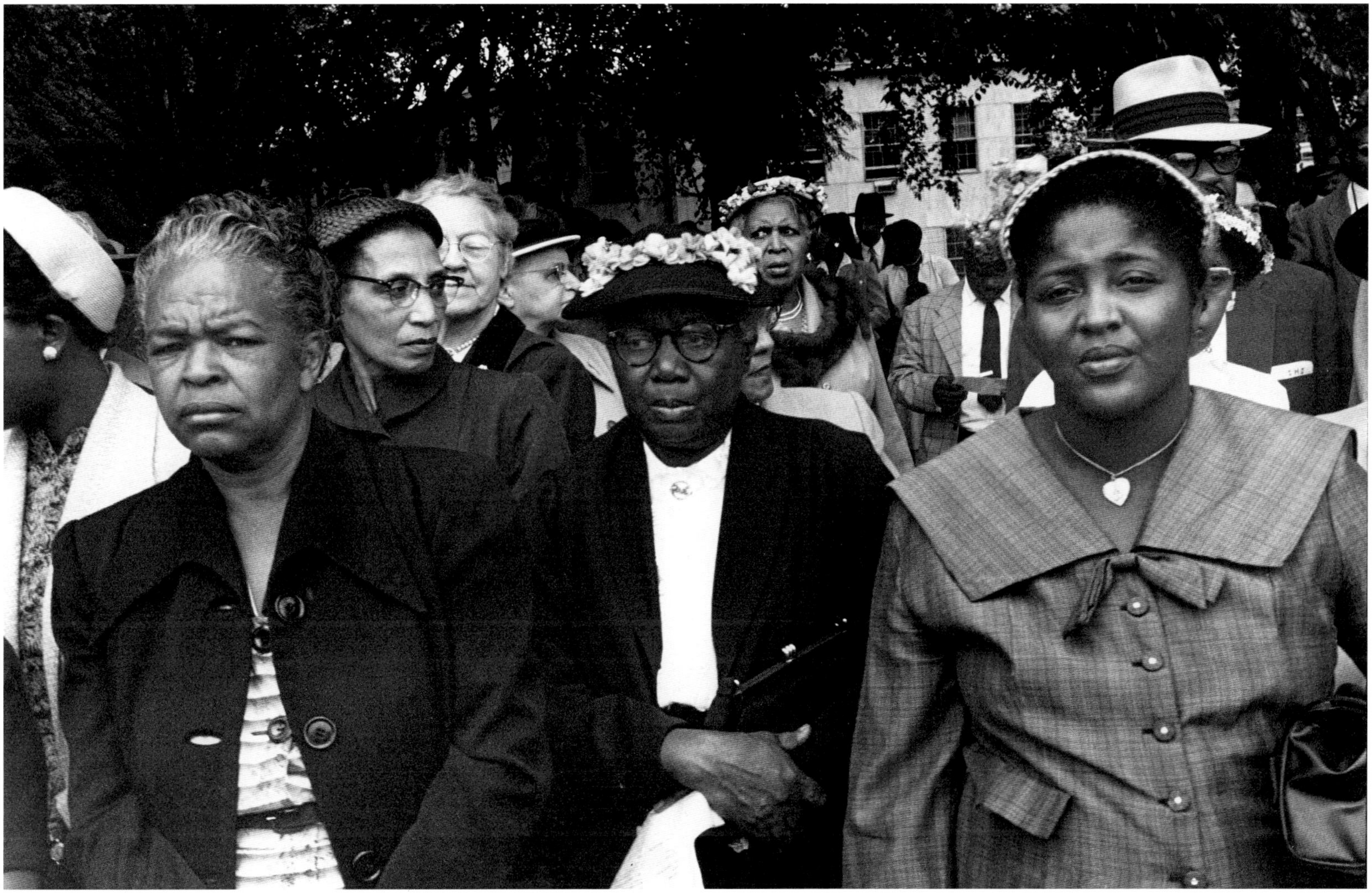

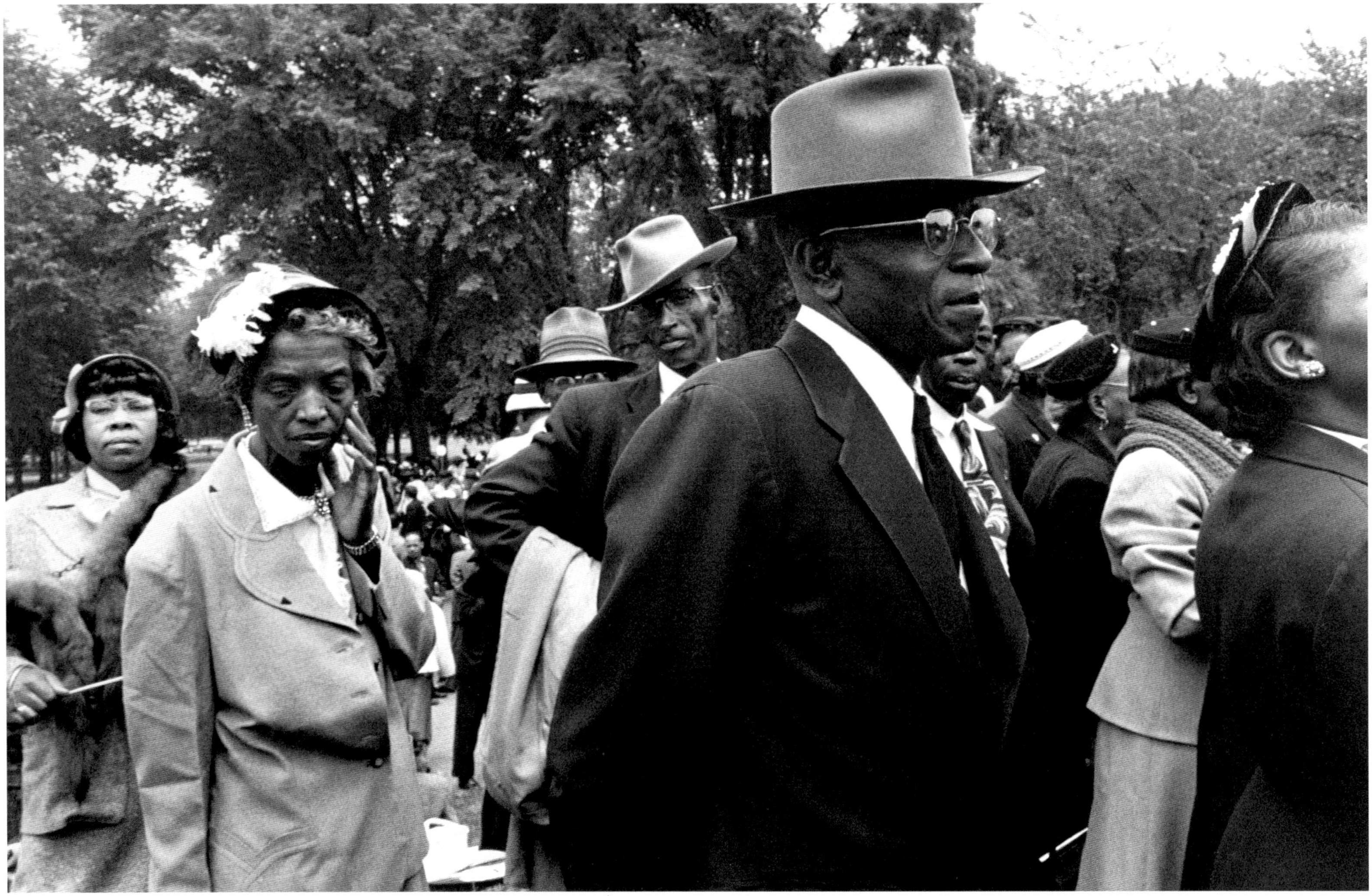

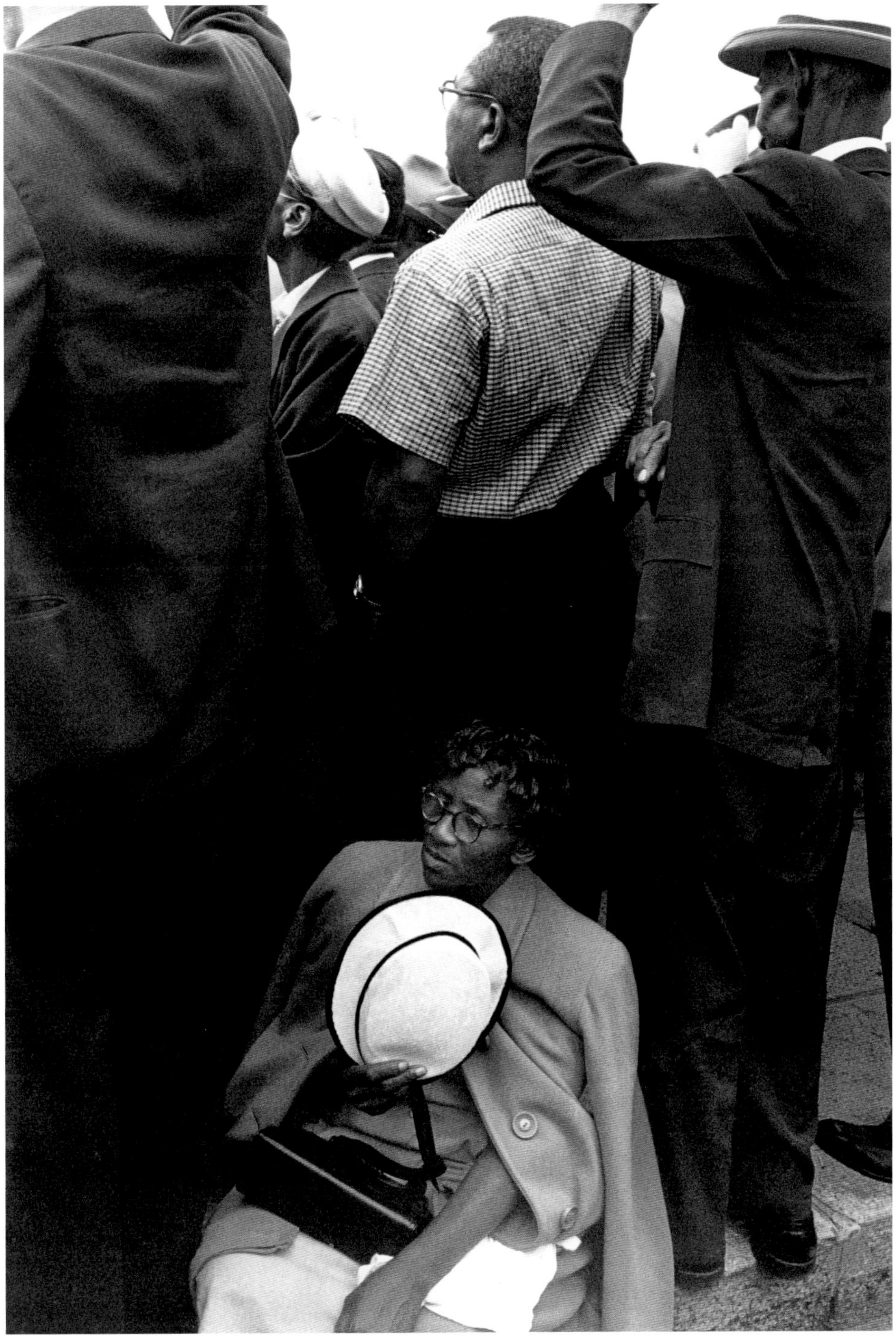

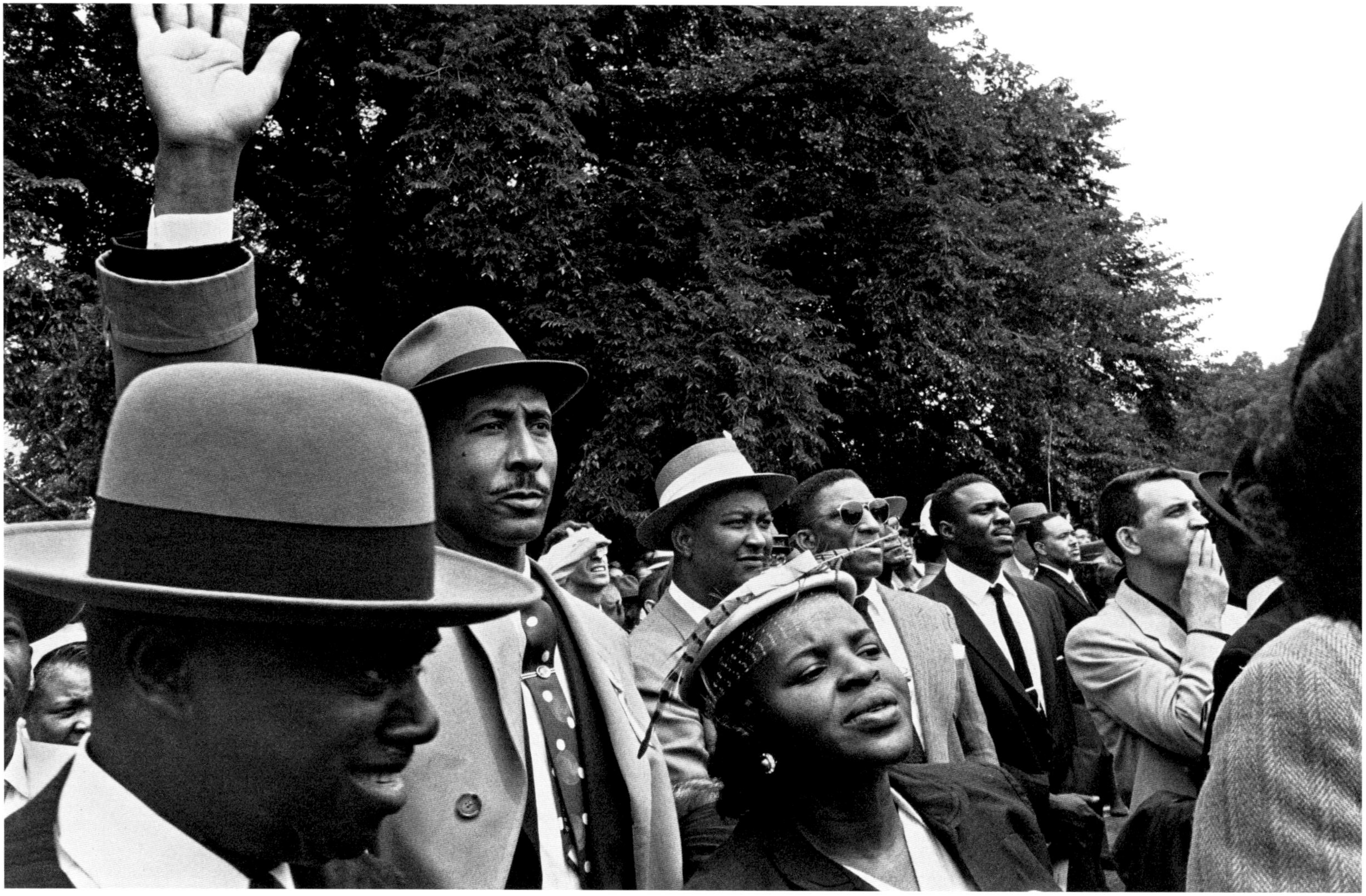

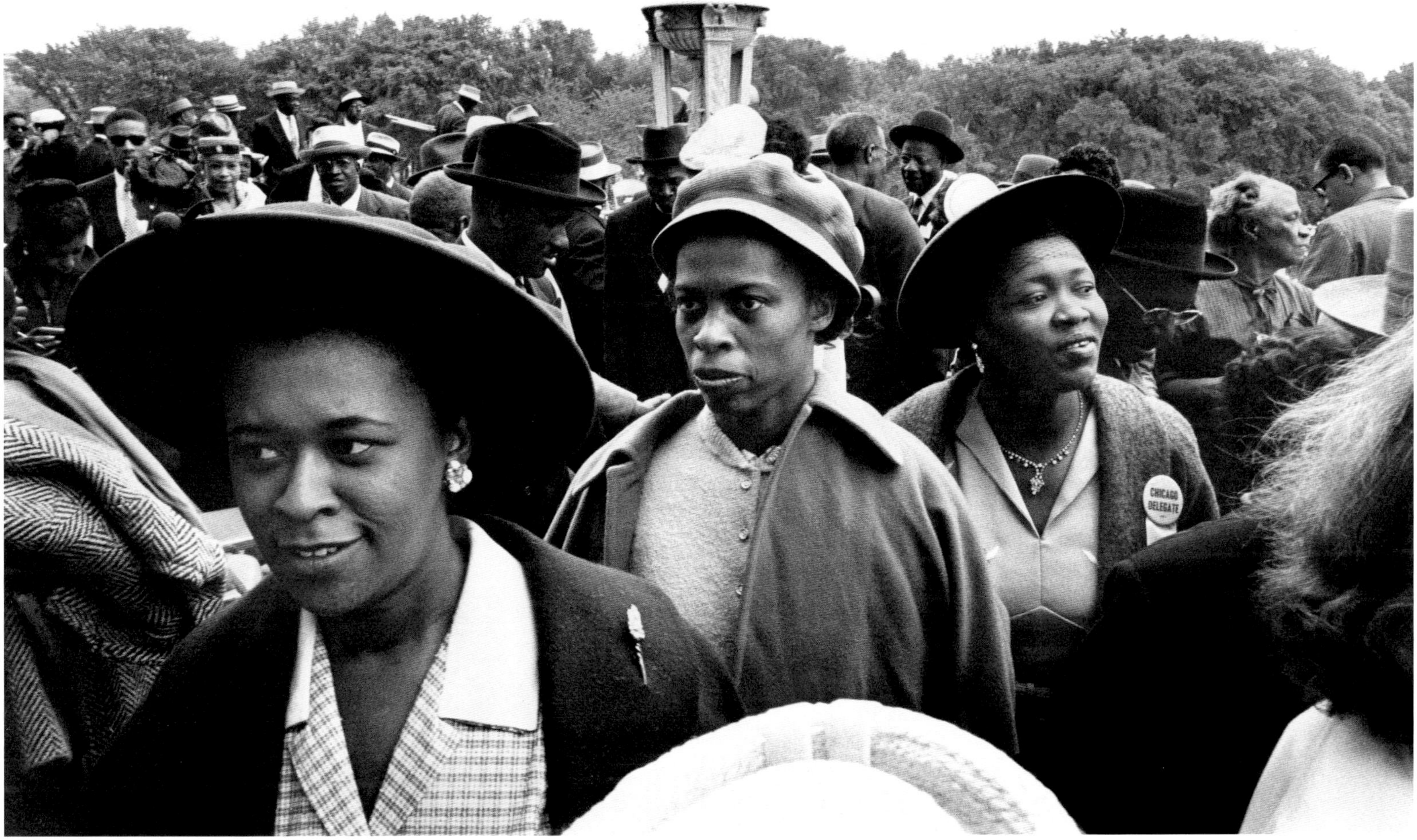
CHICAGO
DELEGATE

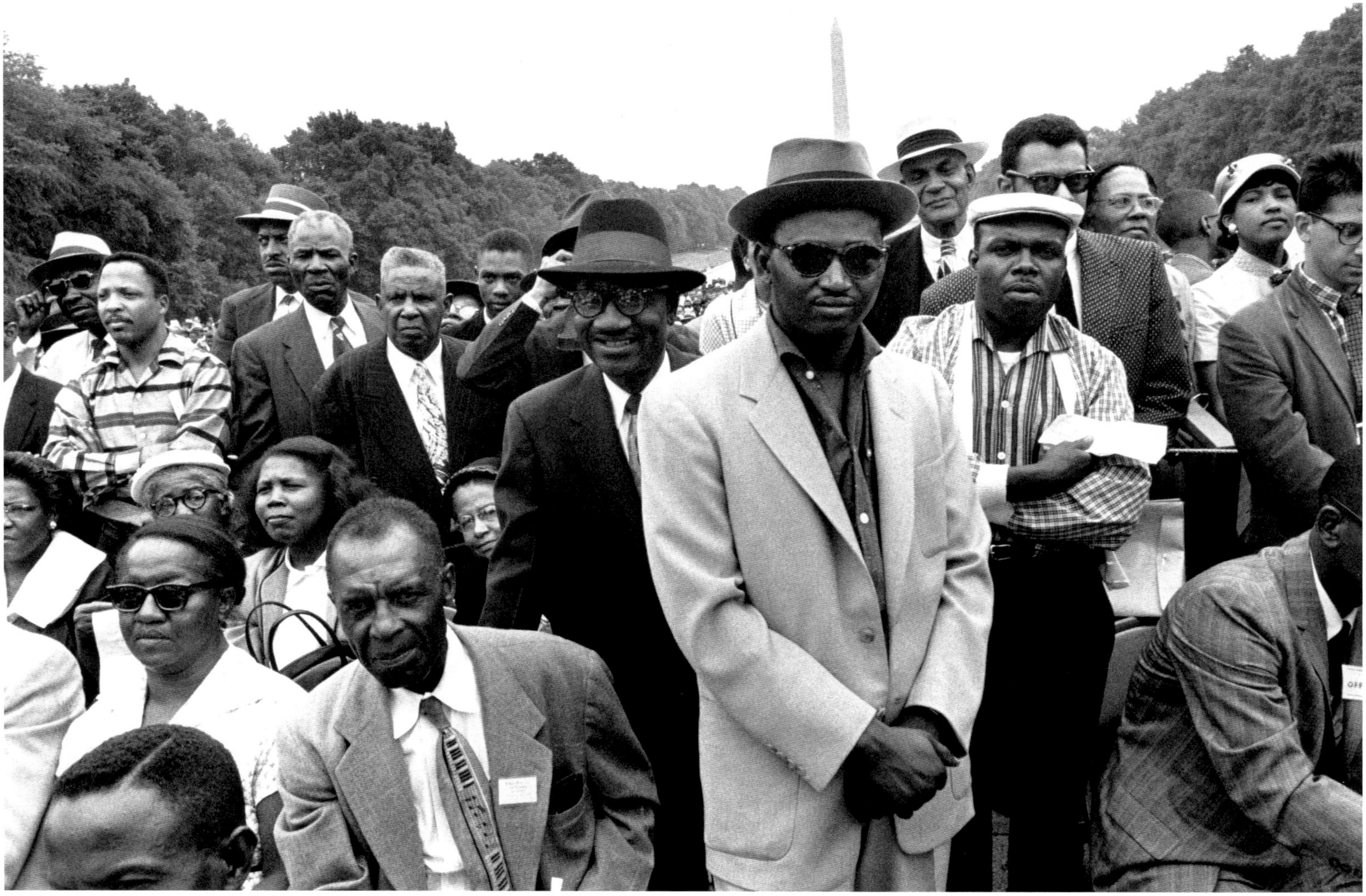

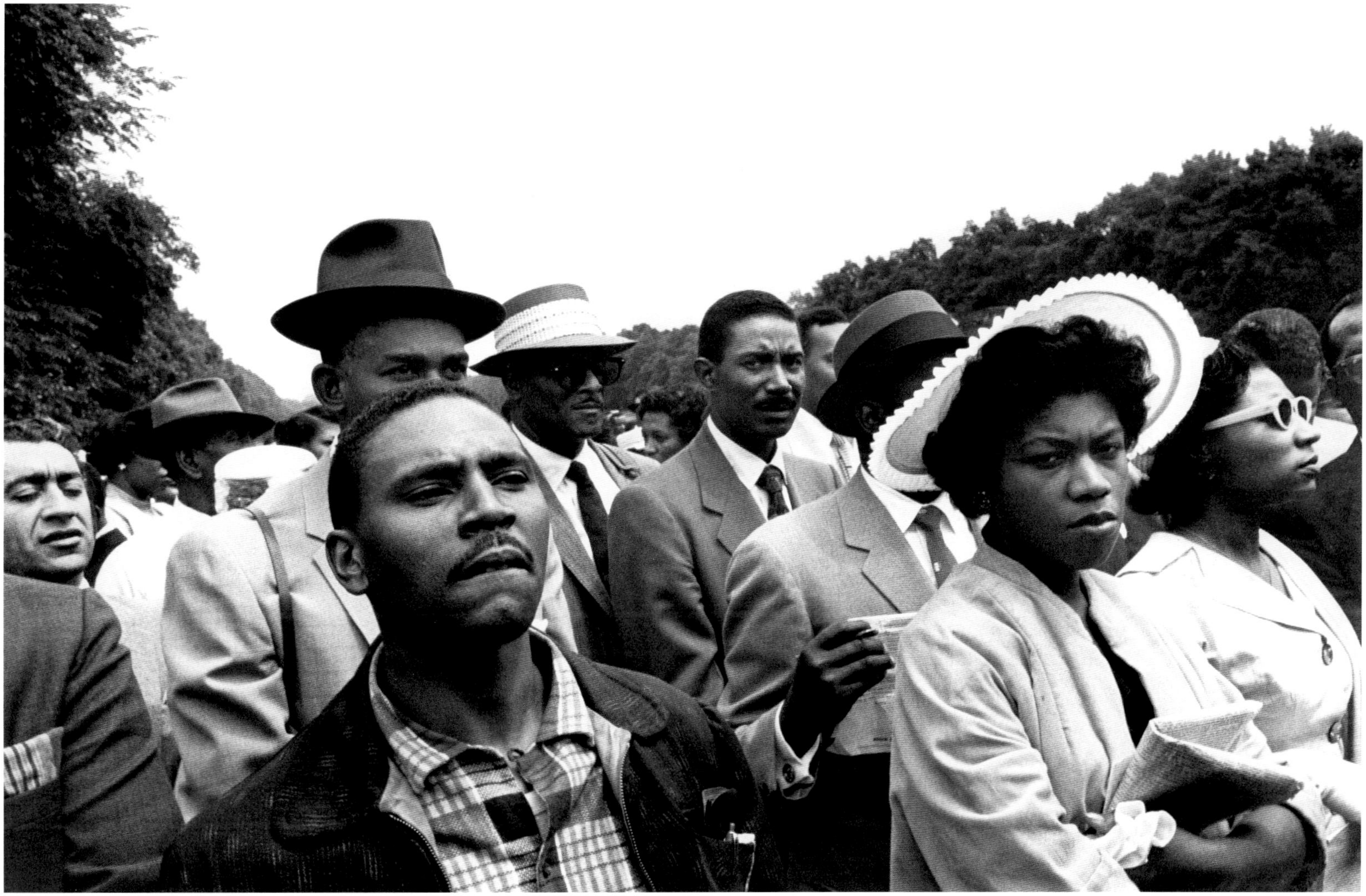

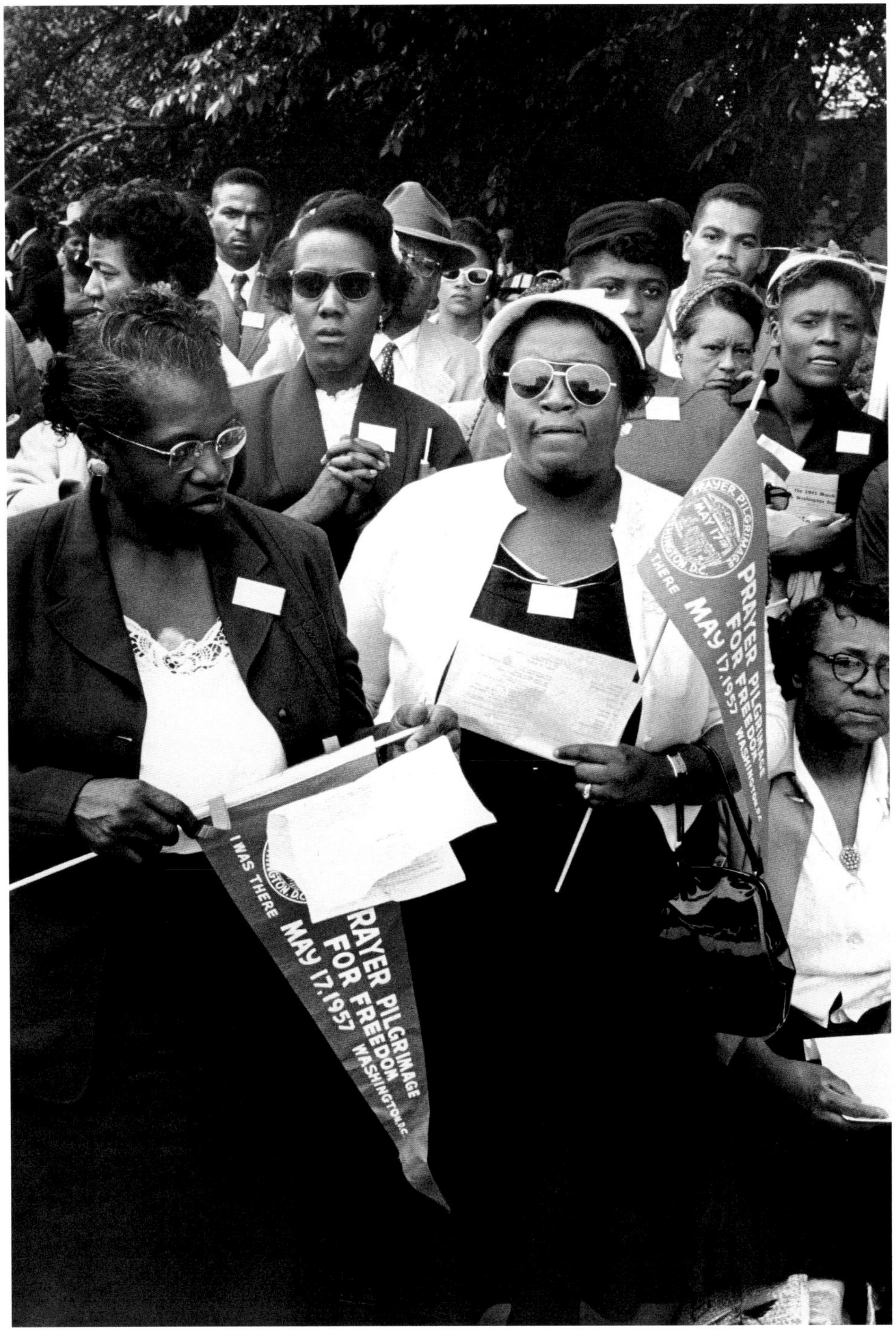
PRAYER PILGRIMAGE
FOR FREEDOM
MAY 17, 1957
WASHINGTON D.C.
I WAS THERE
PRAYER PILGRIMAGE
FOR FREEDOM
MAY 17, 1957
WASHINGTON D.C.
I WAS THERE

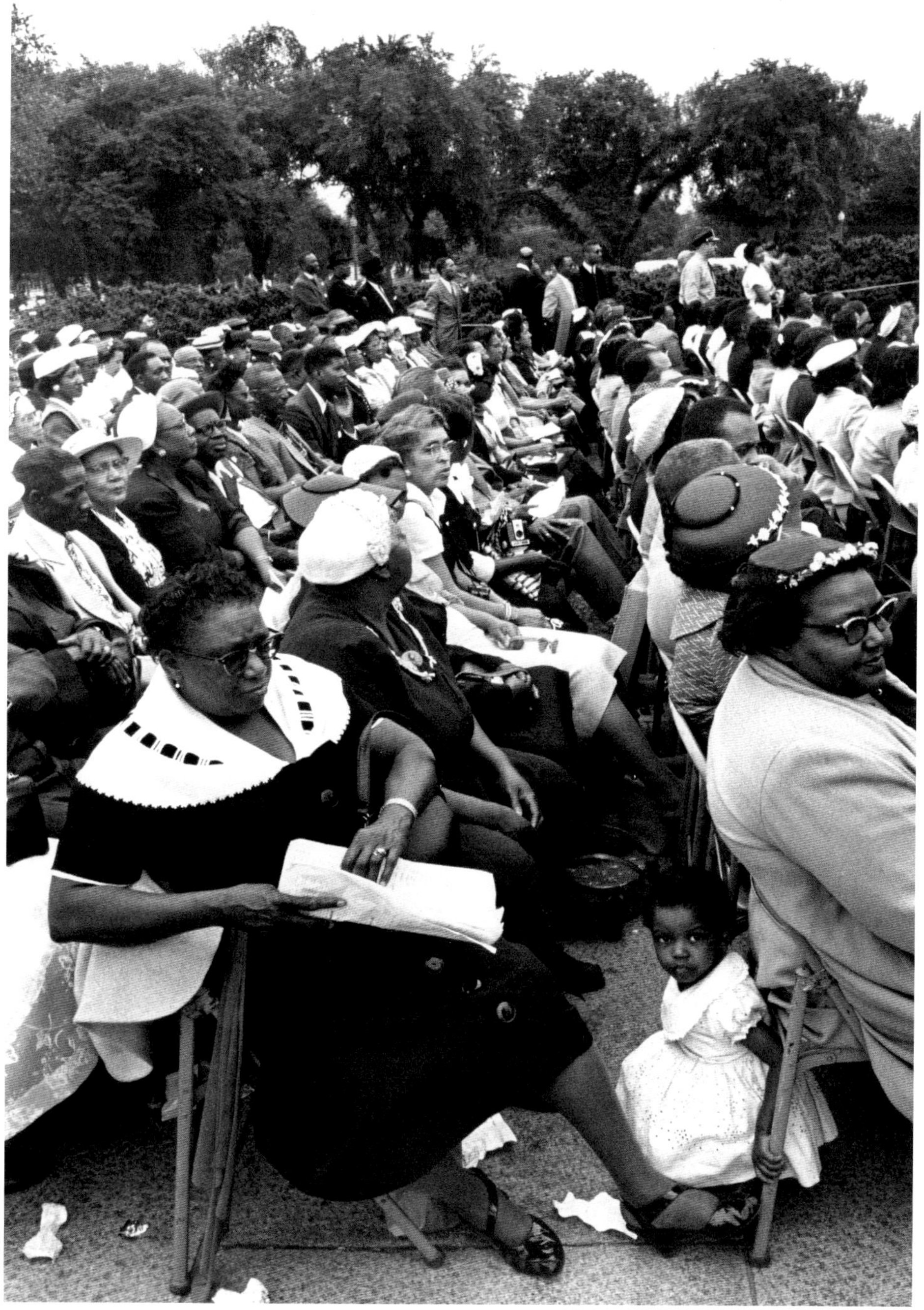

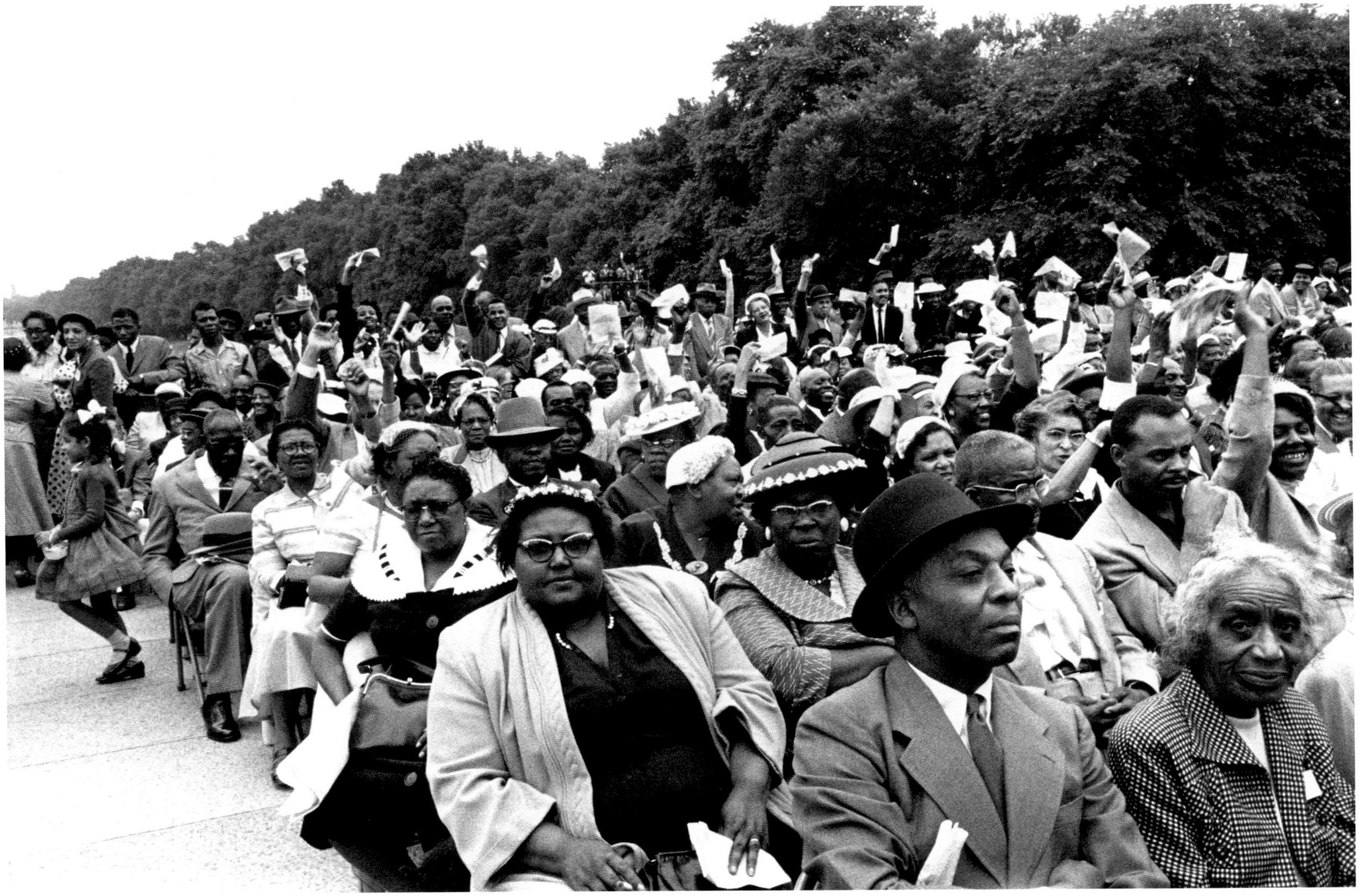

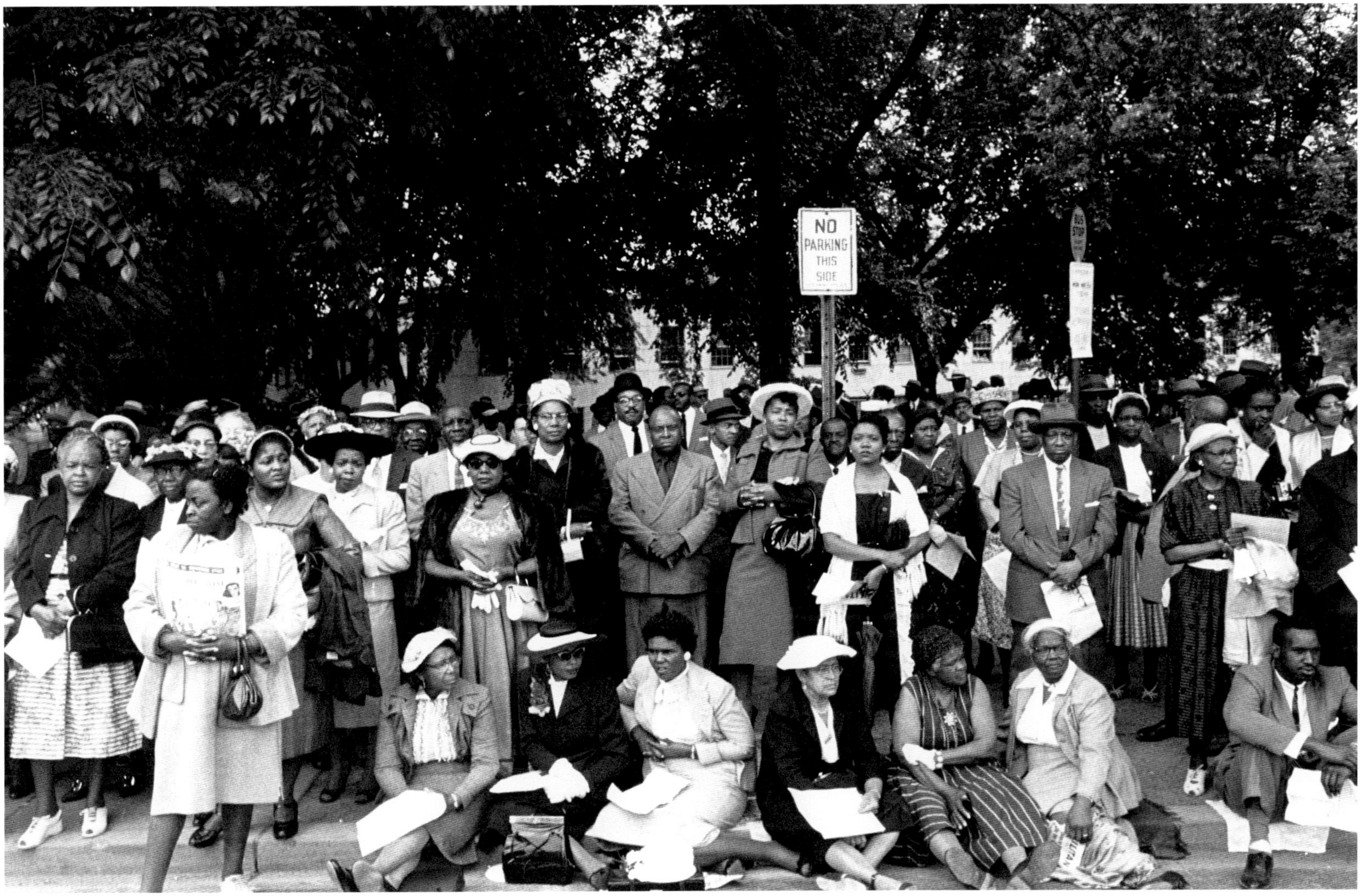
NO
PARKING
THIS
SIDE

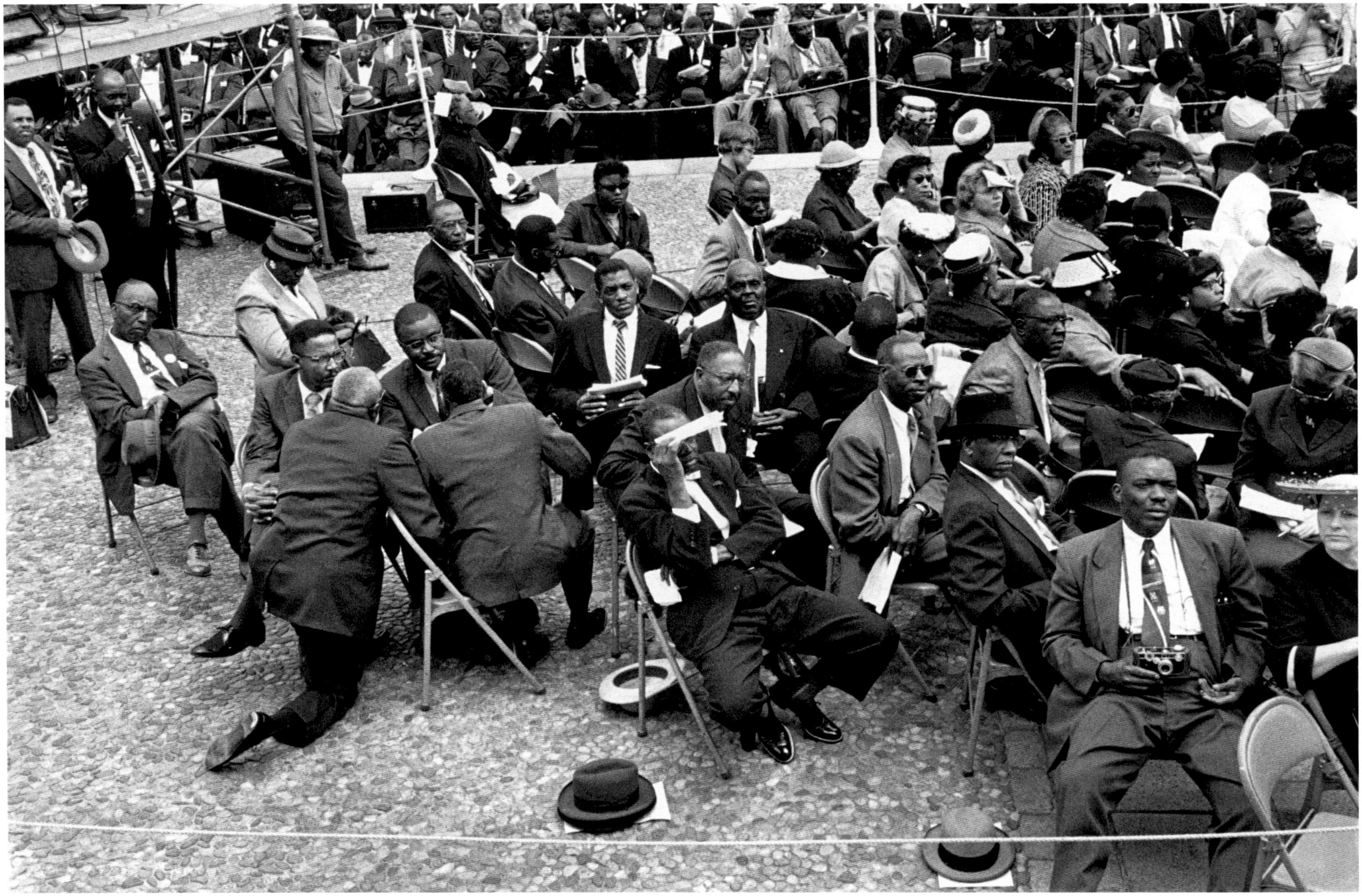

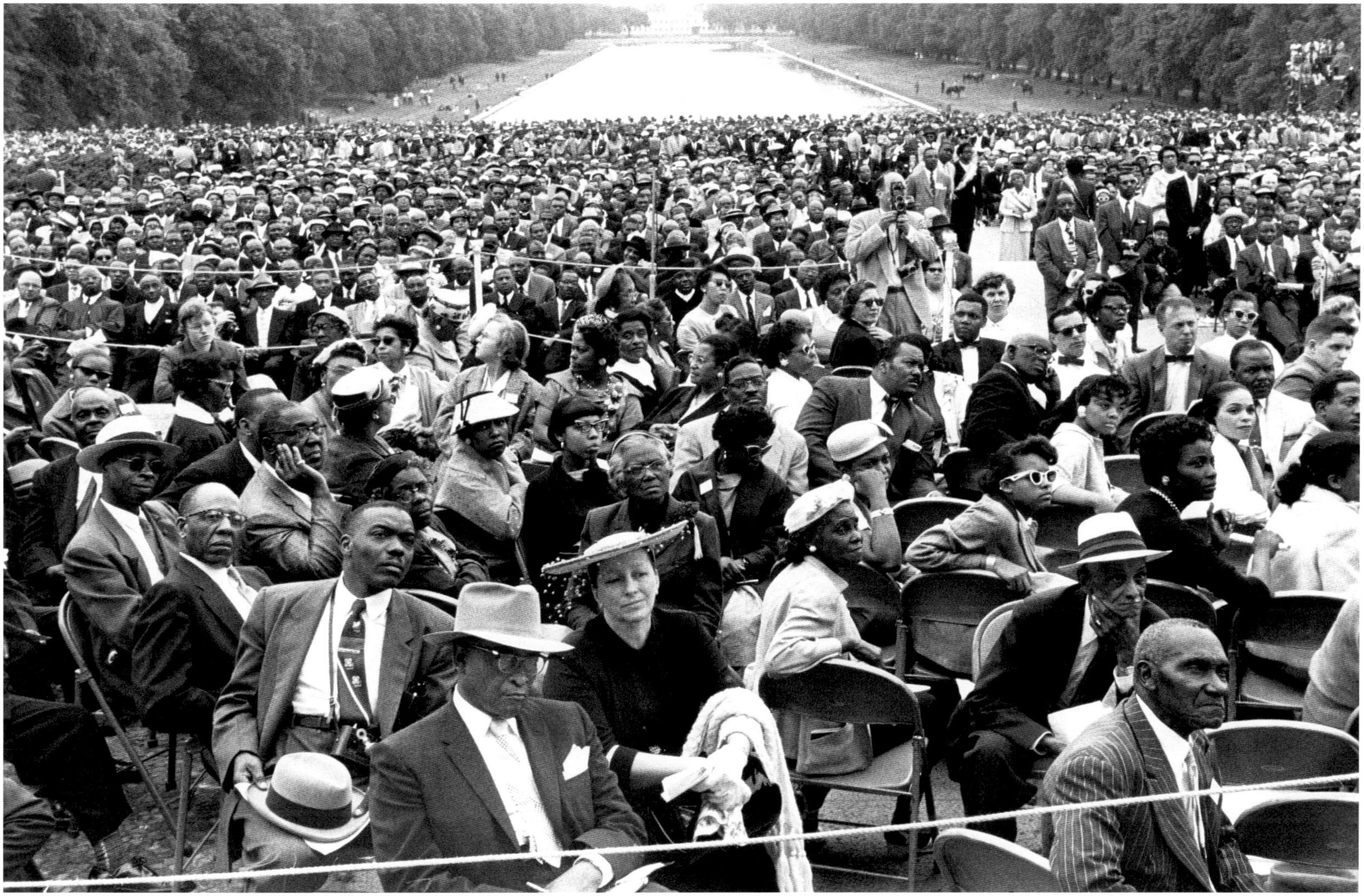

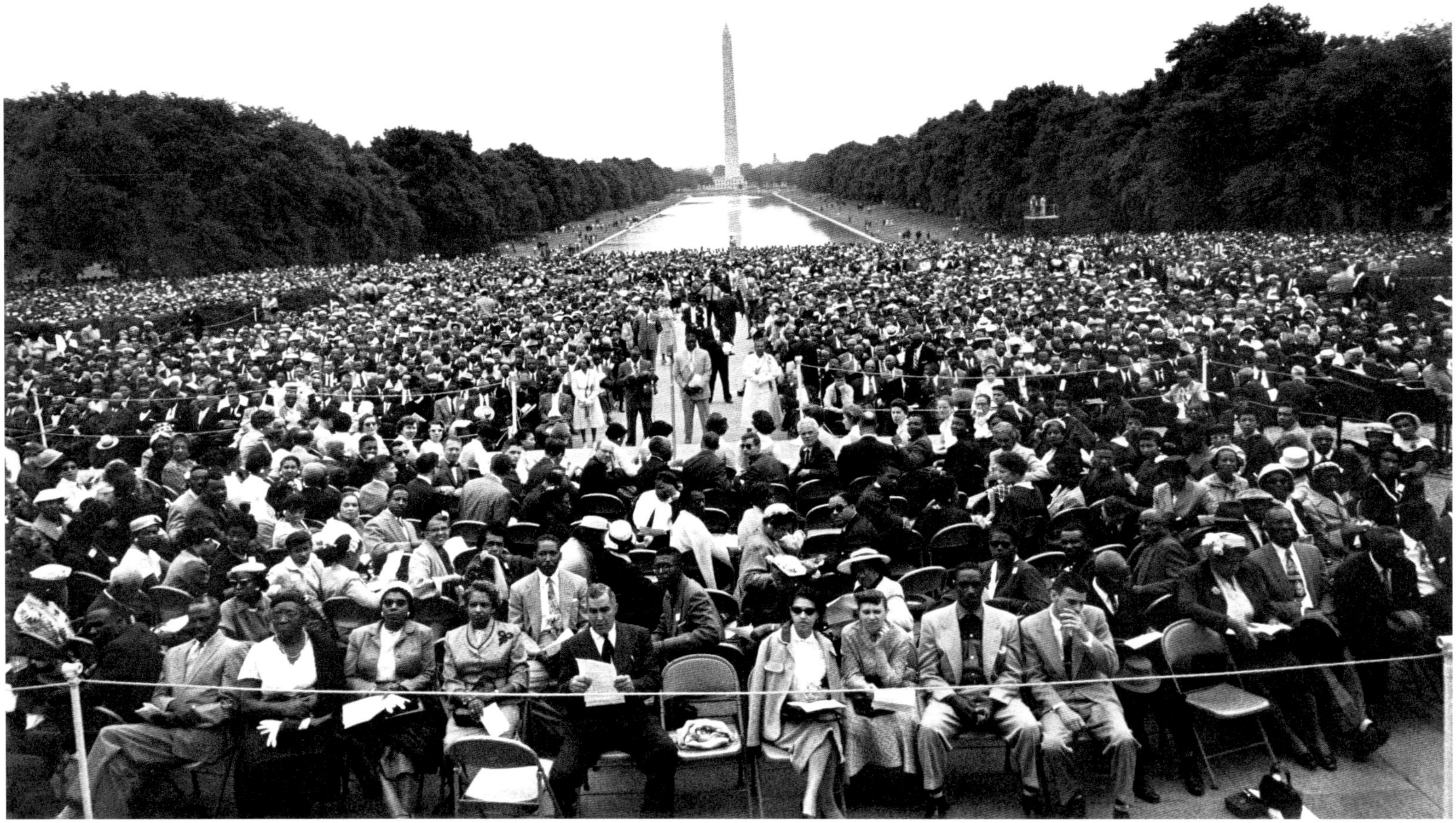

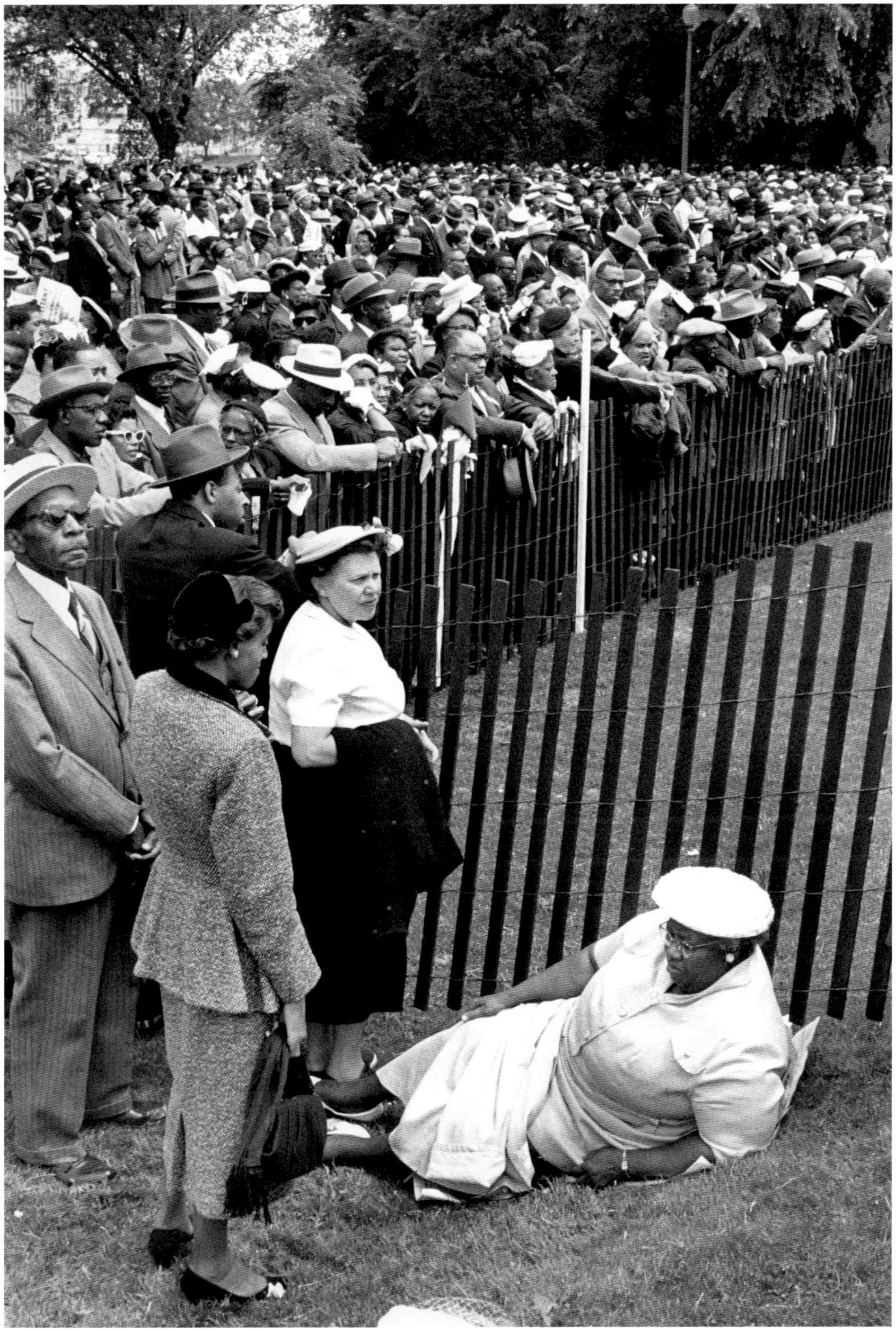

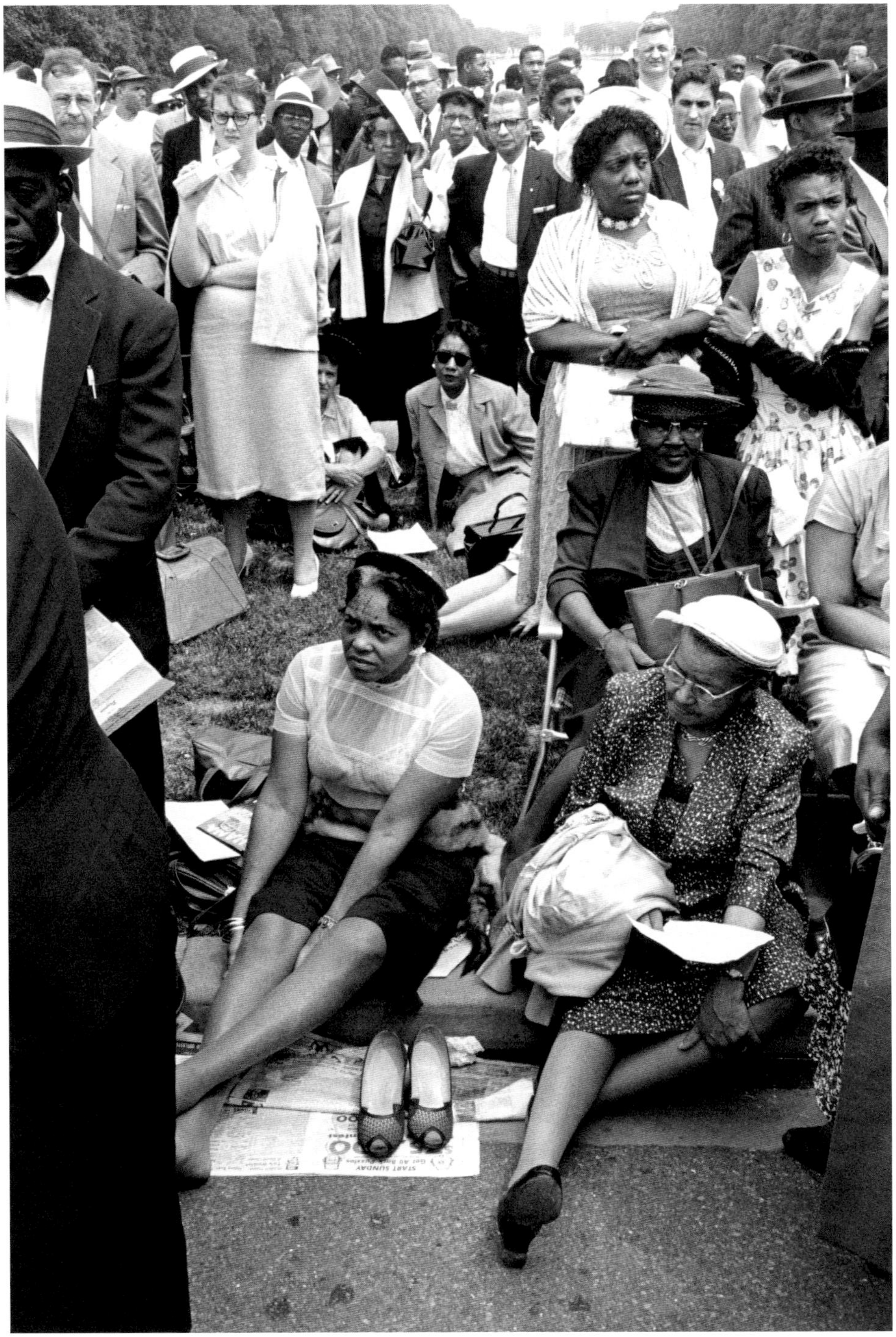
START SUNDAY

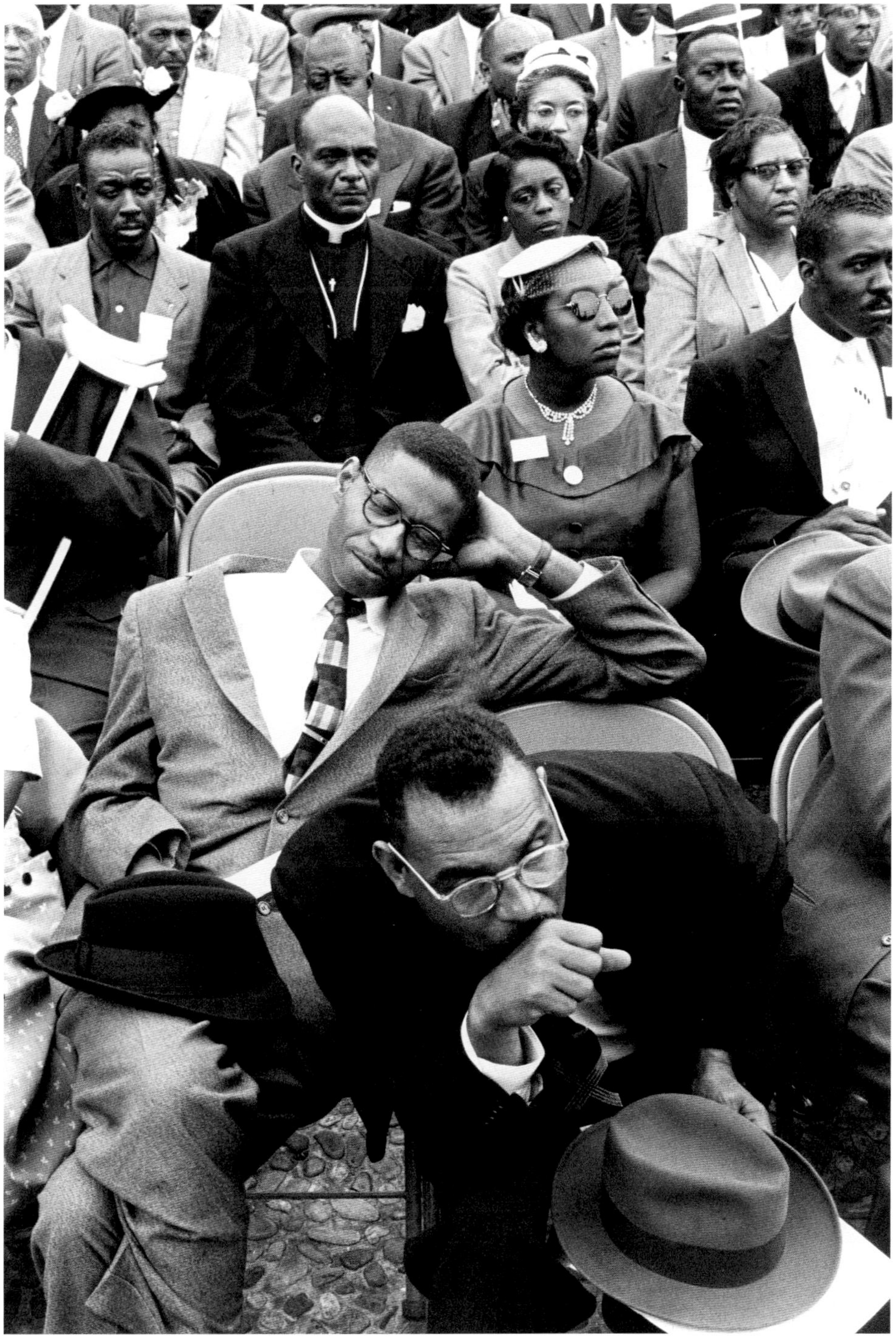

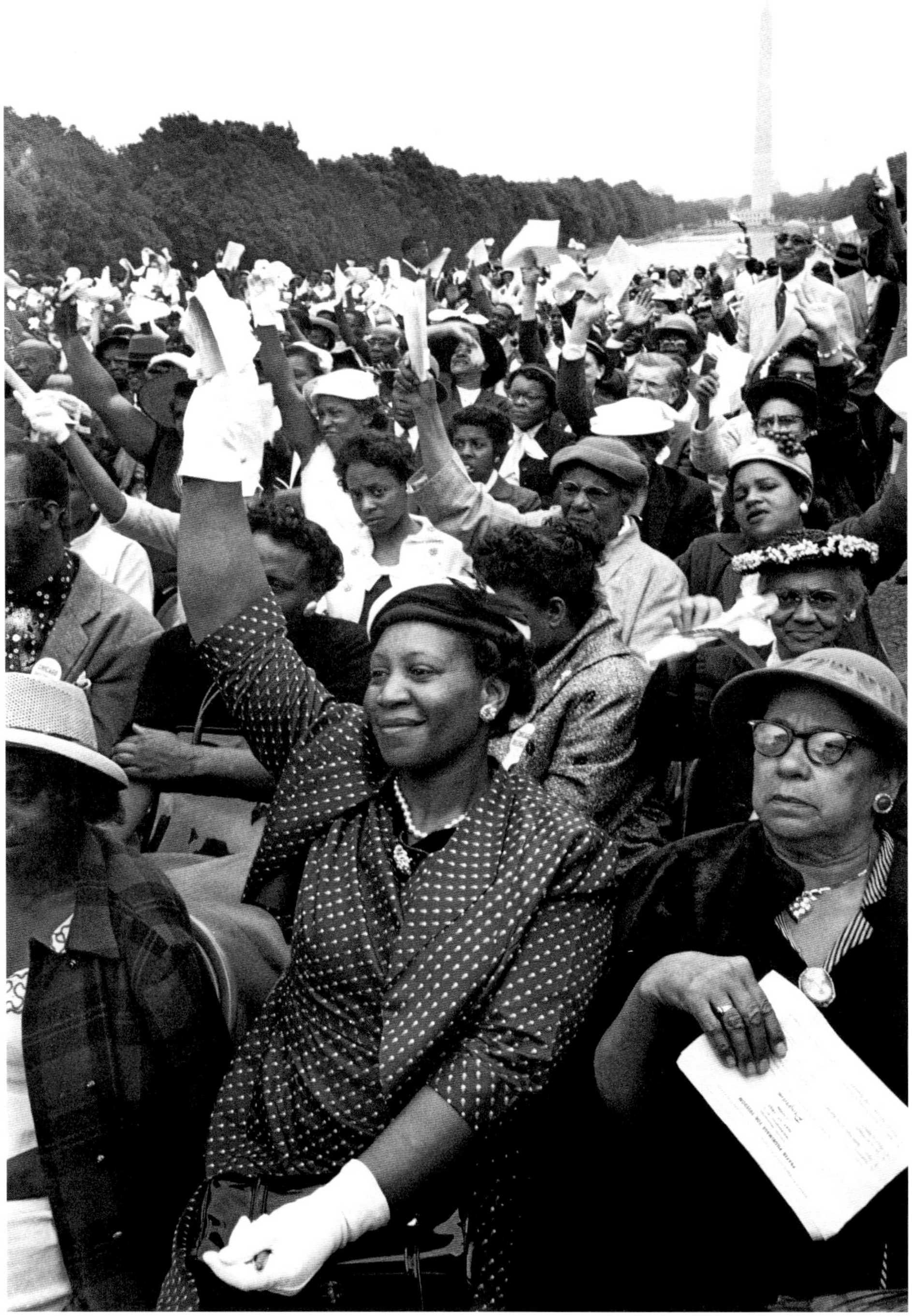

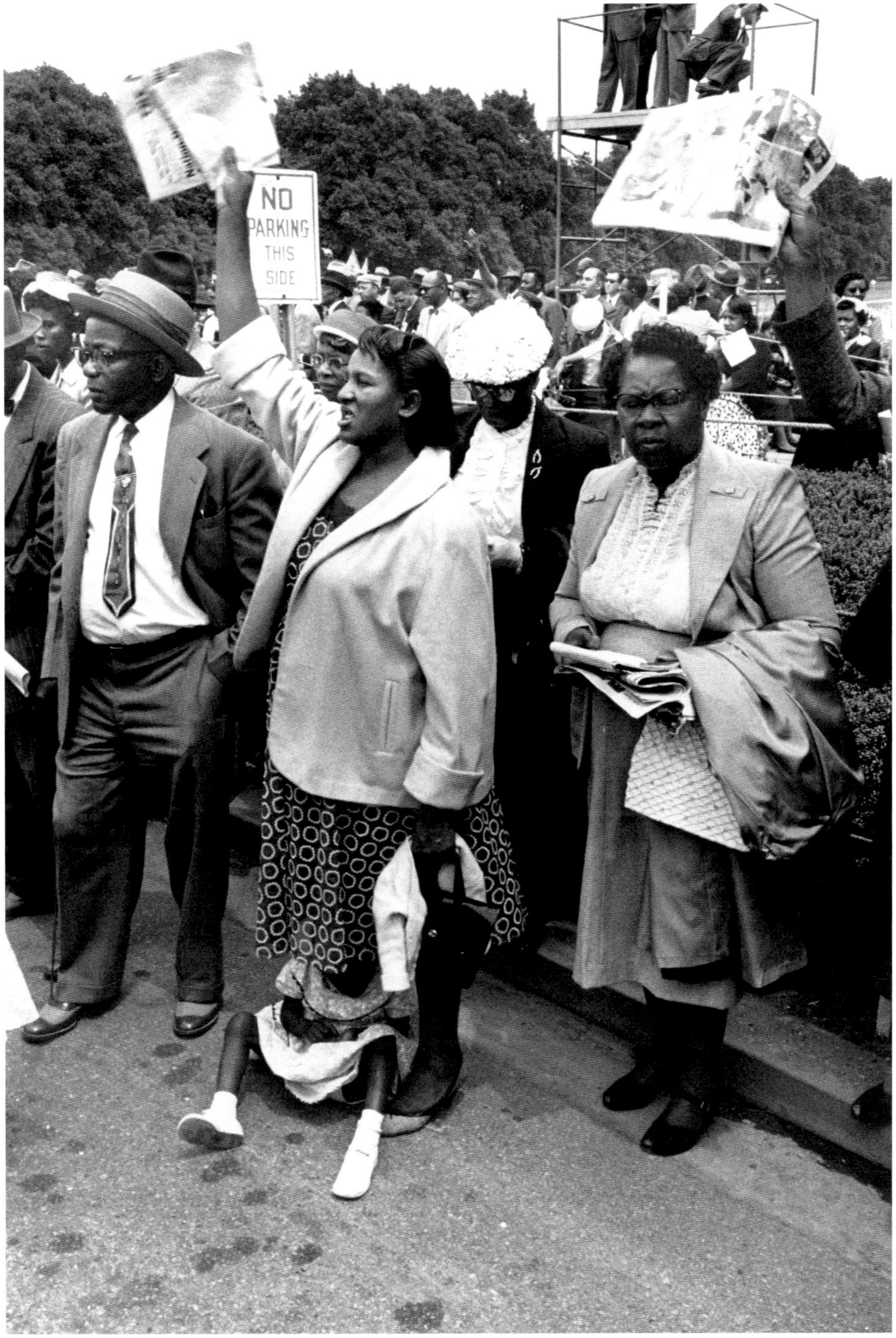
NO
PARKING
THIS
SIDE

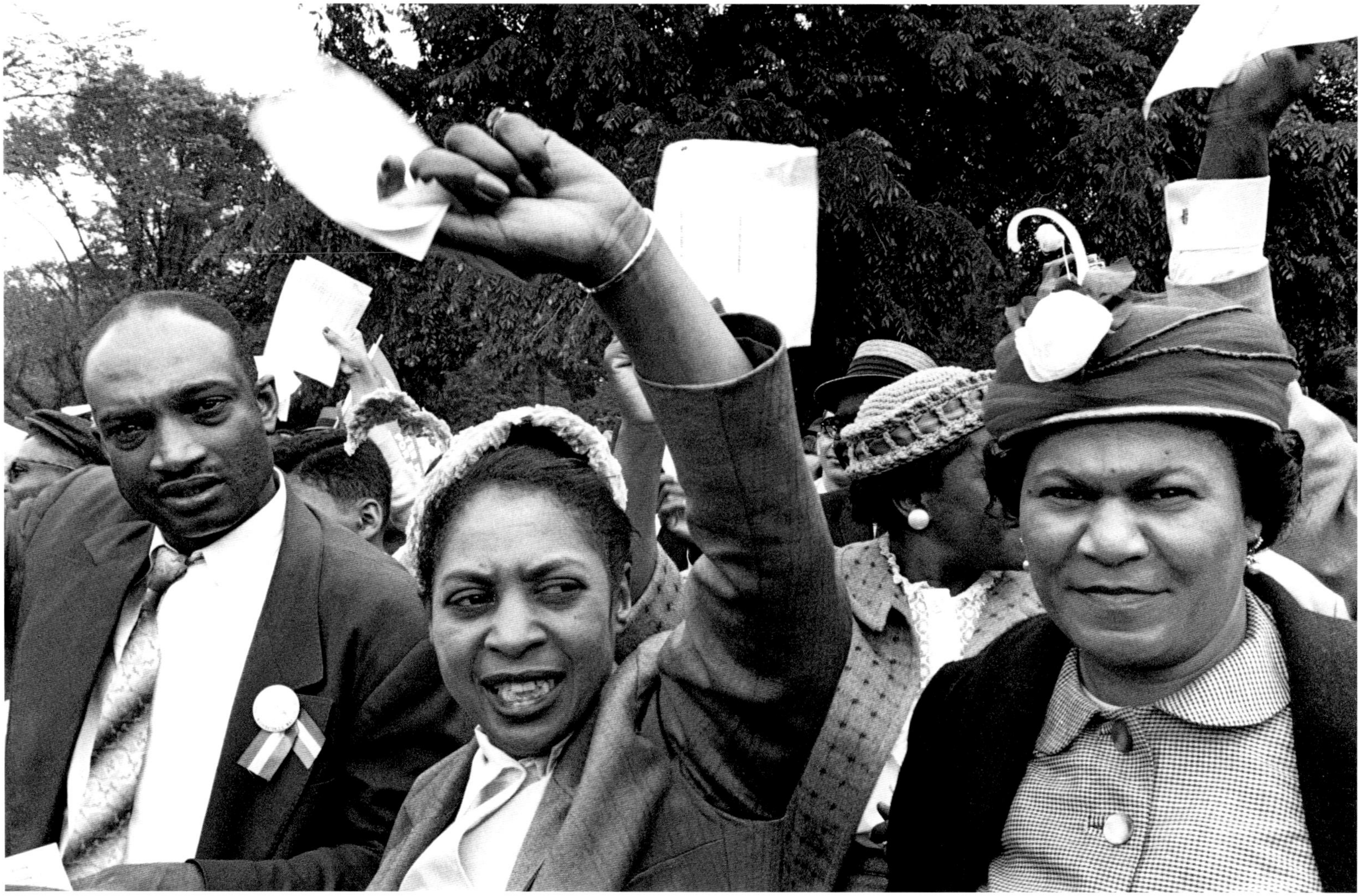

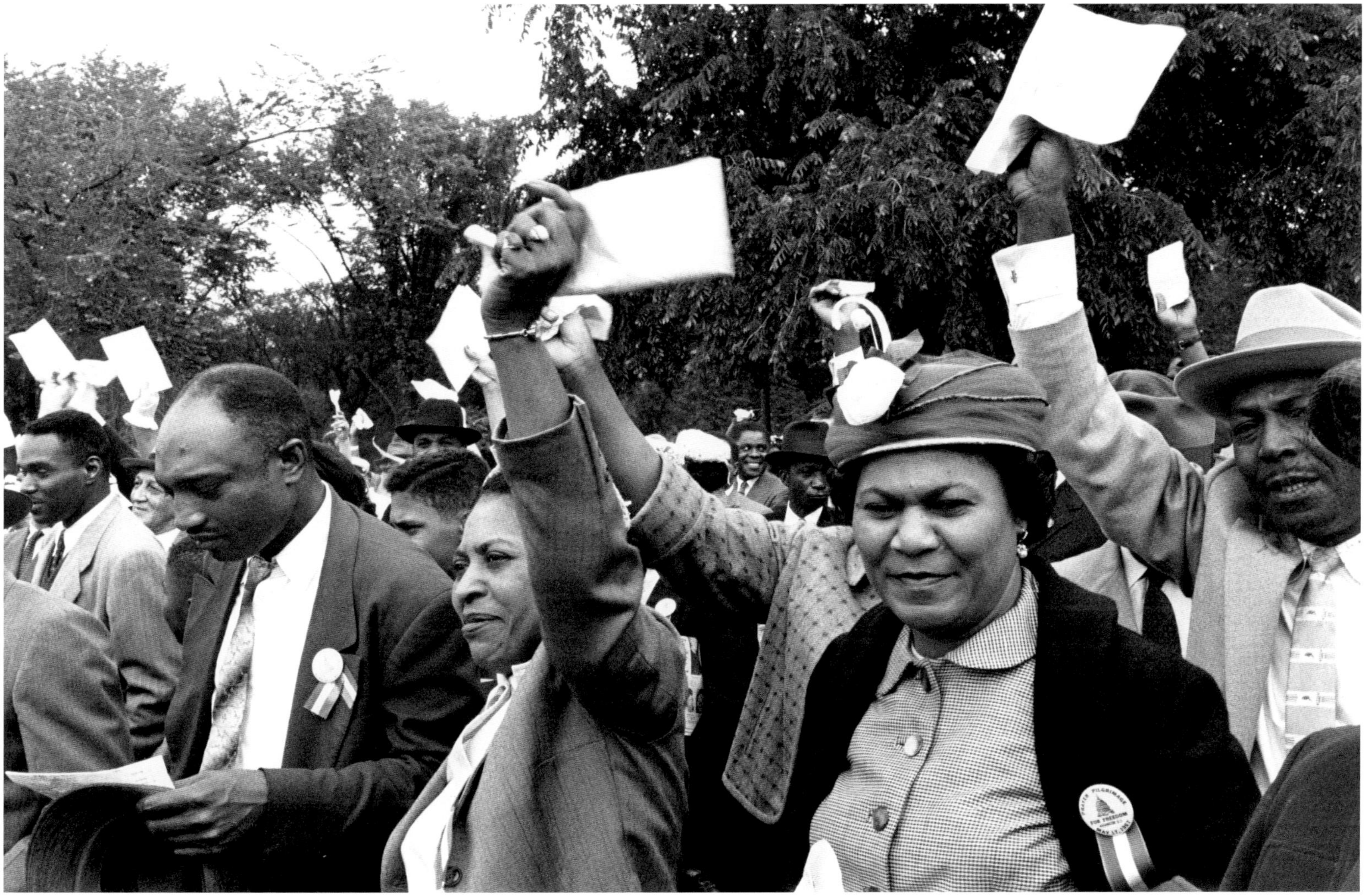
PRAYER PILGRIMAGE
FOR FREEDOM
MAY 17, 1957

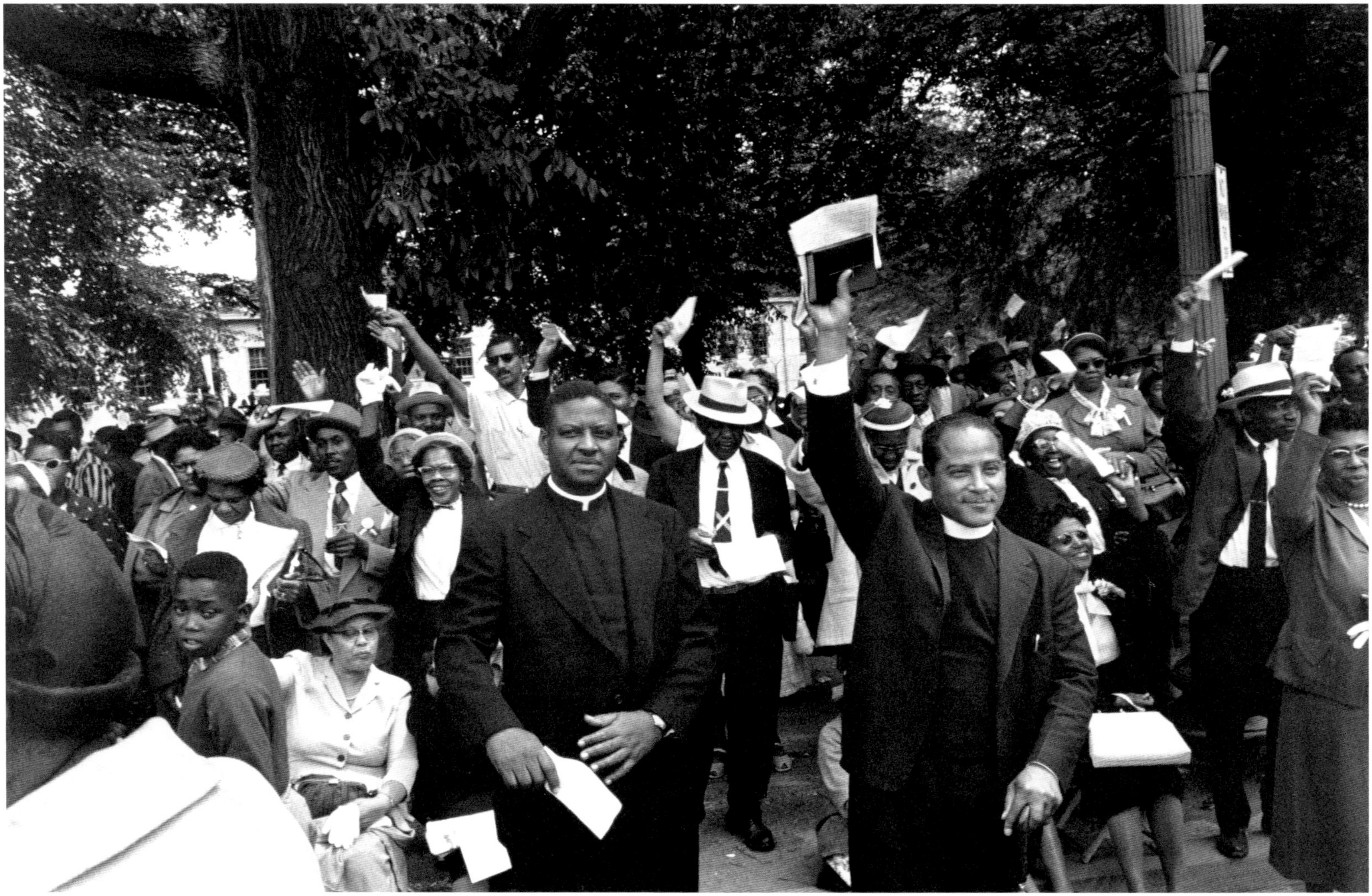

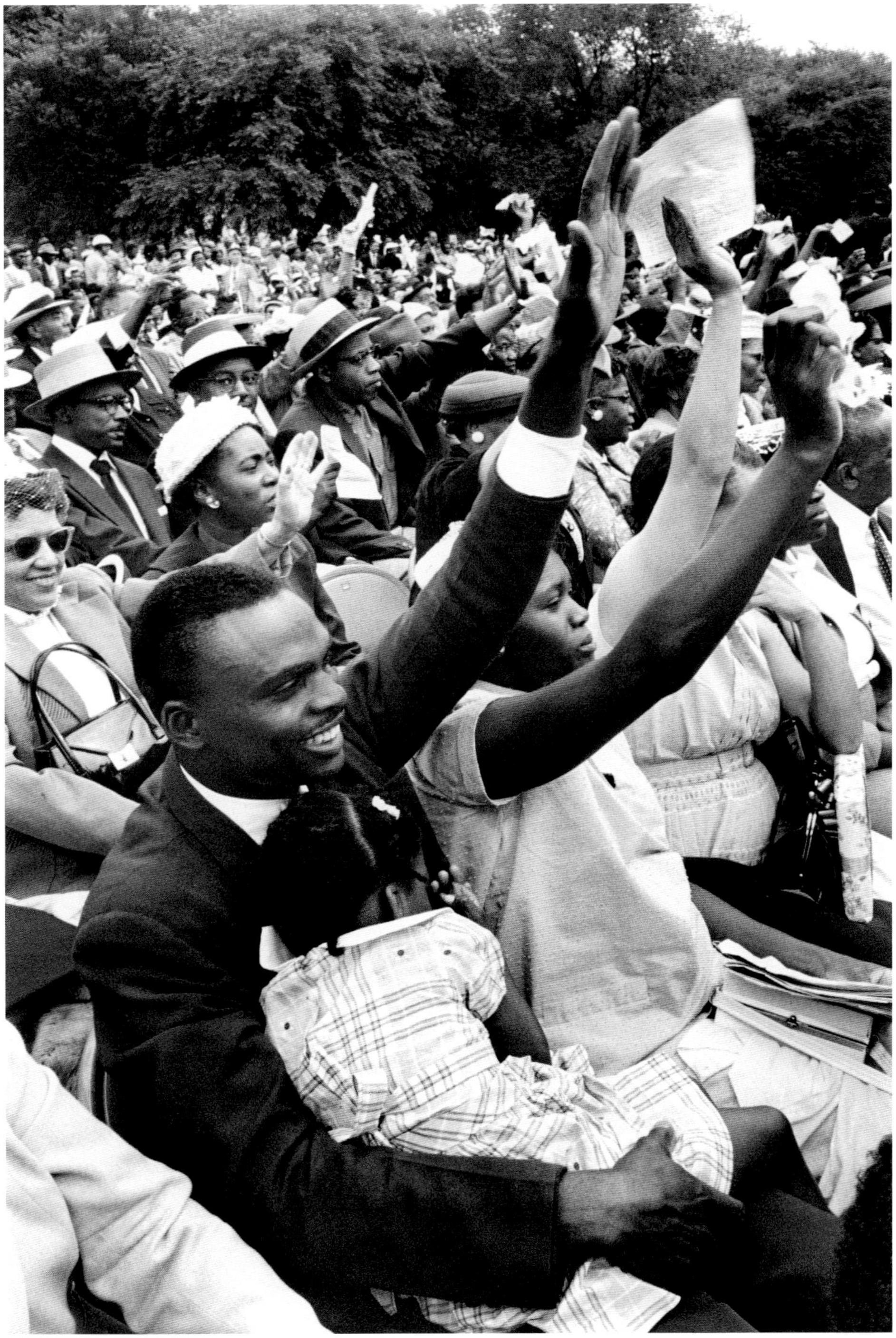

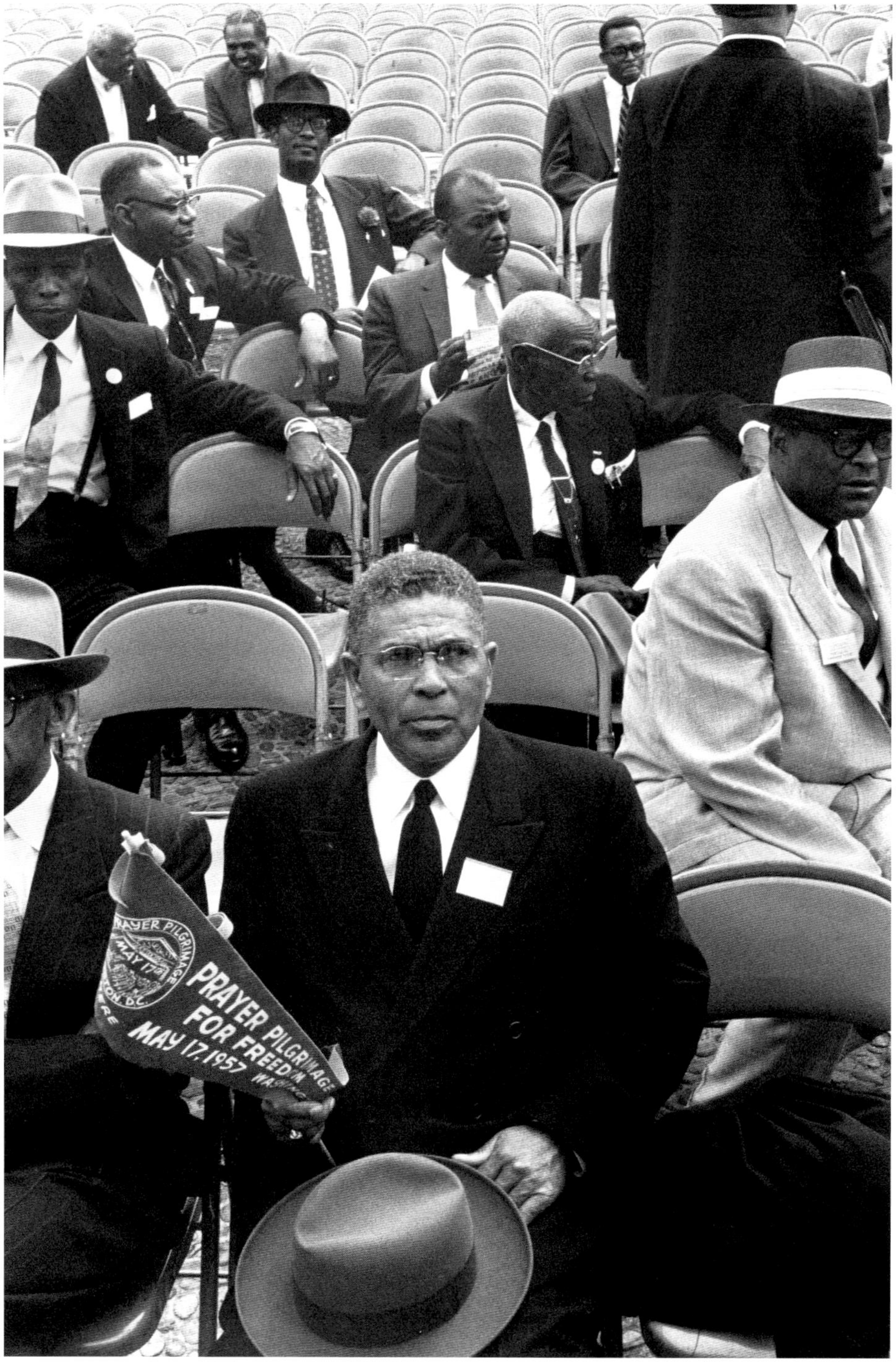
PRAYER PILGRIMAGE
MAY 17, 1957

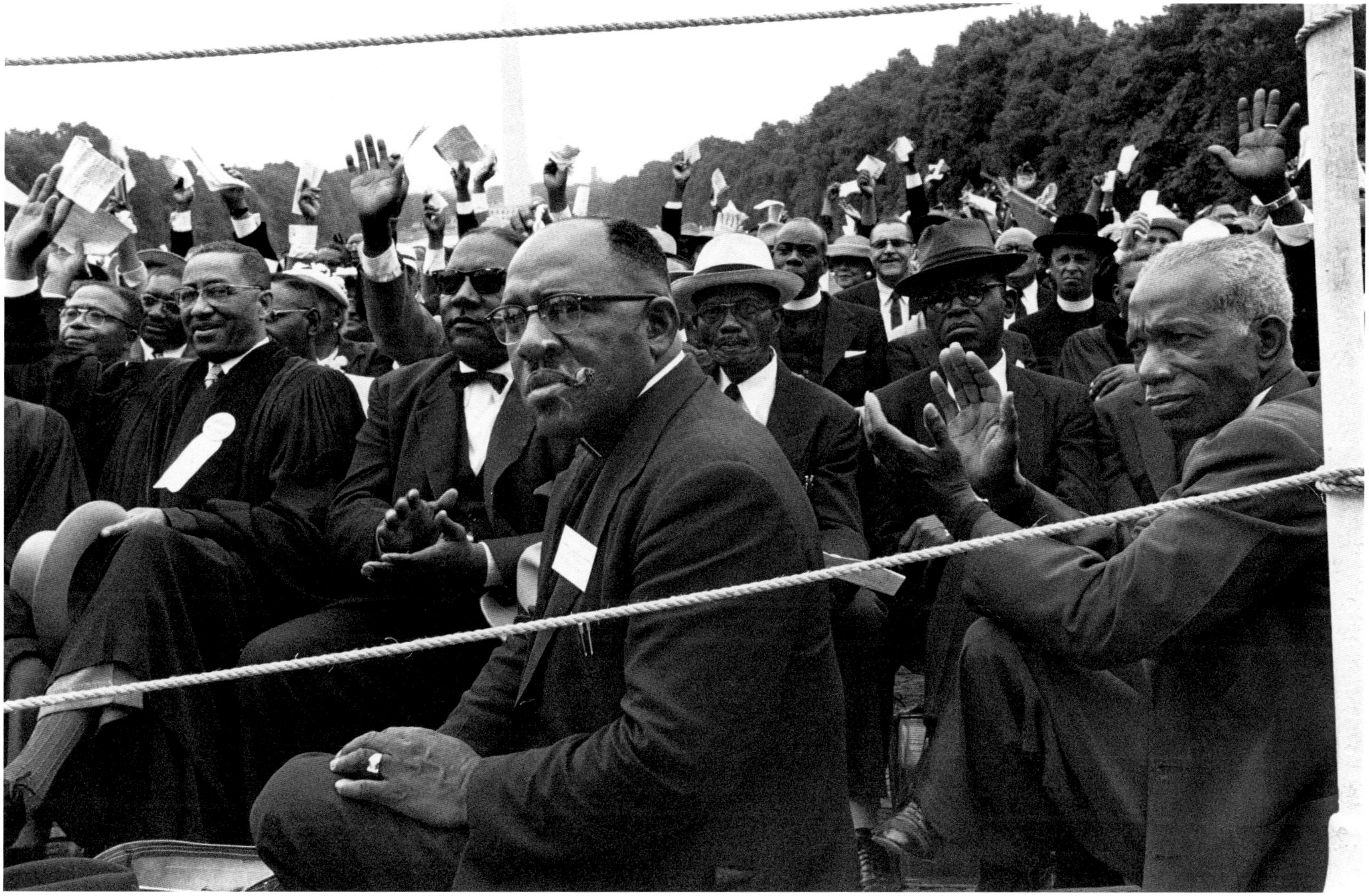

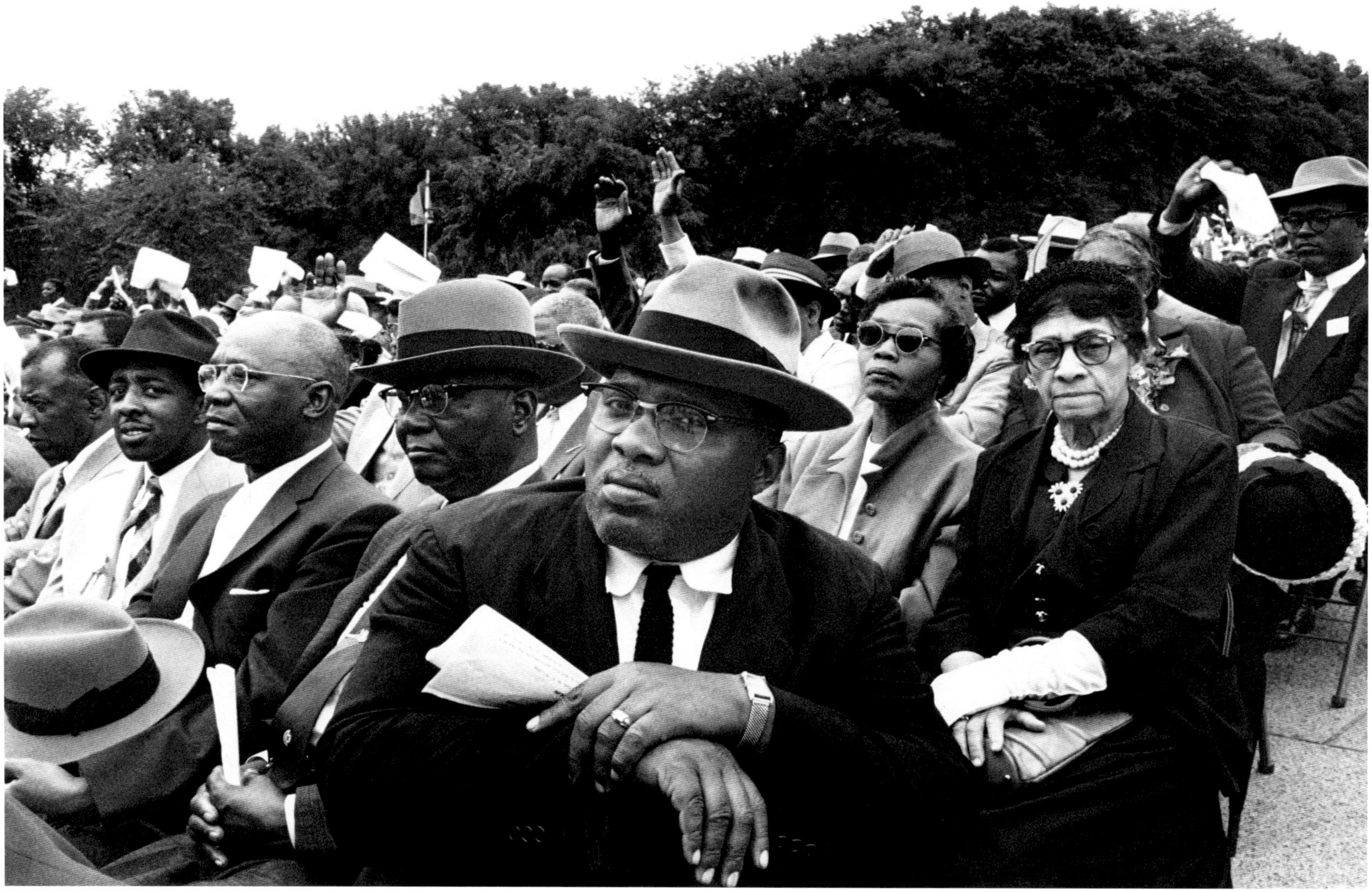

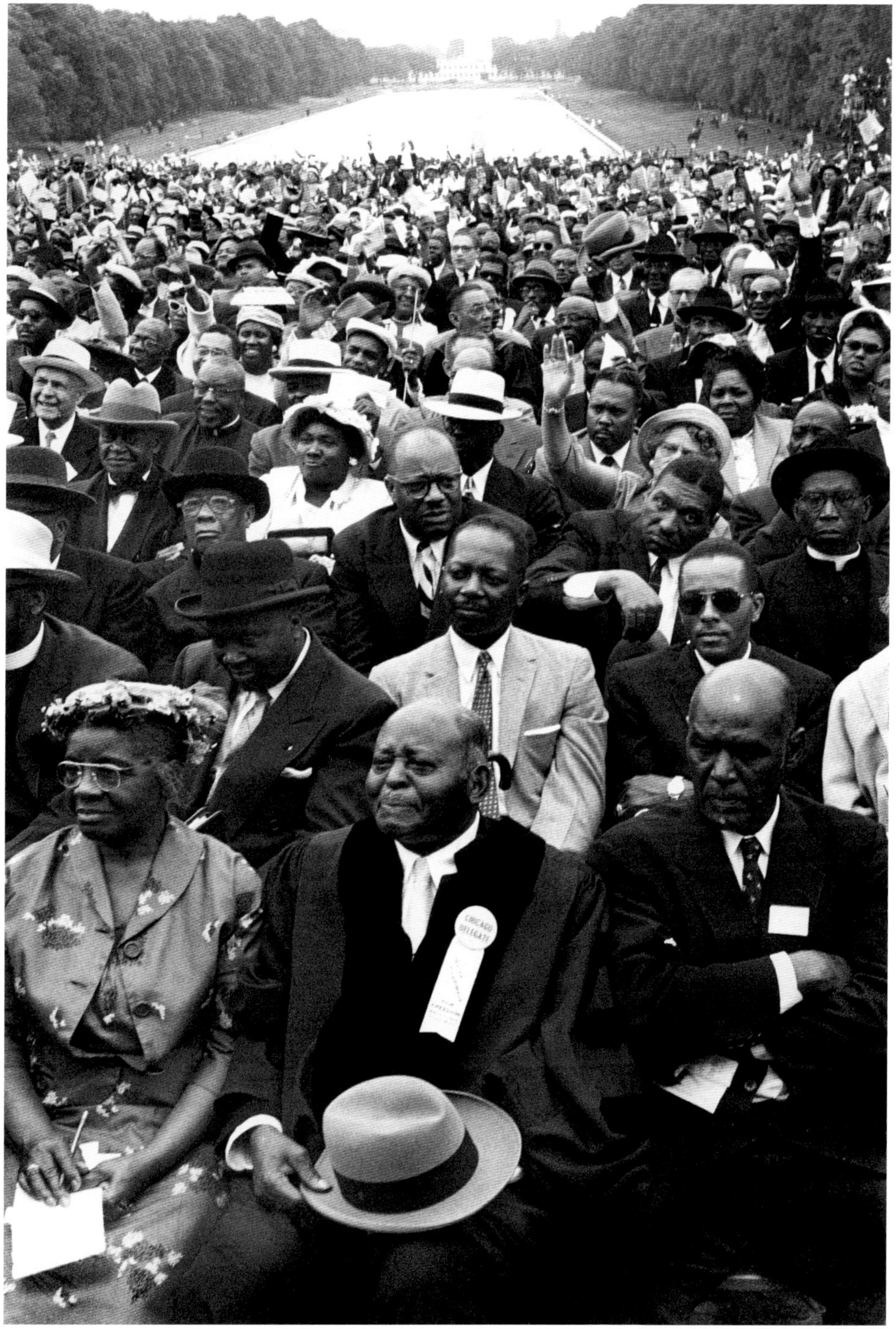

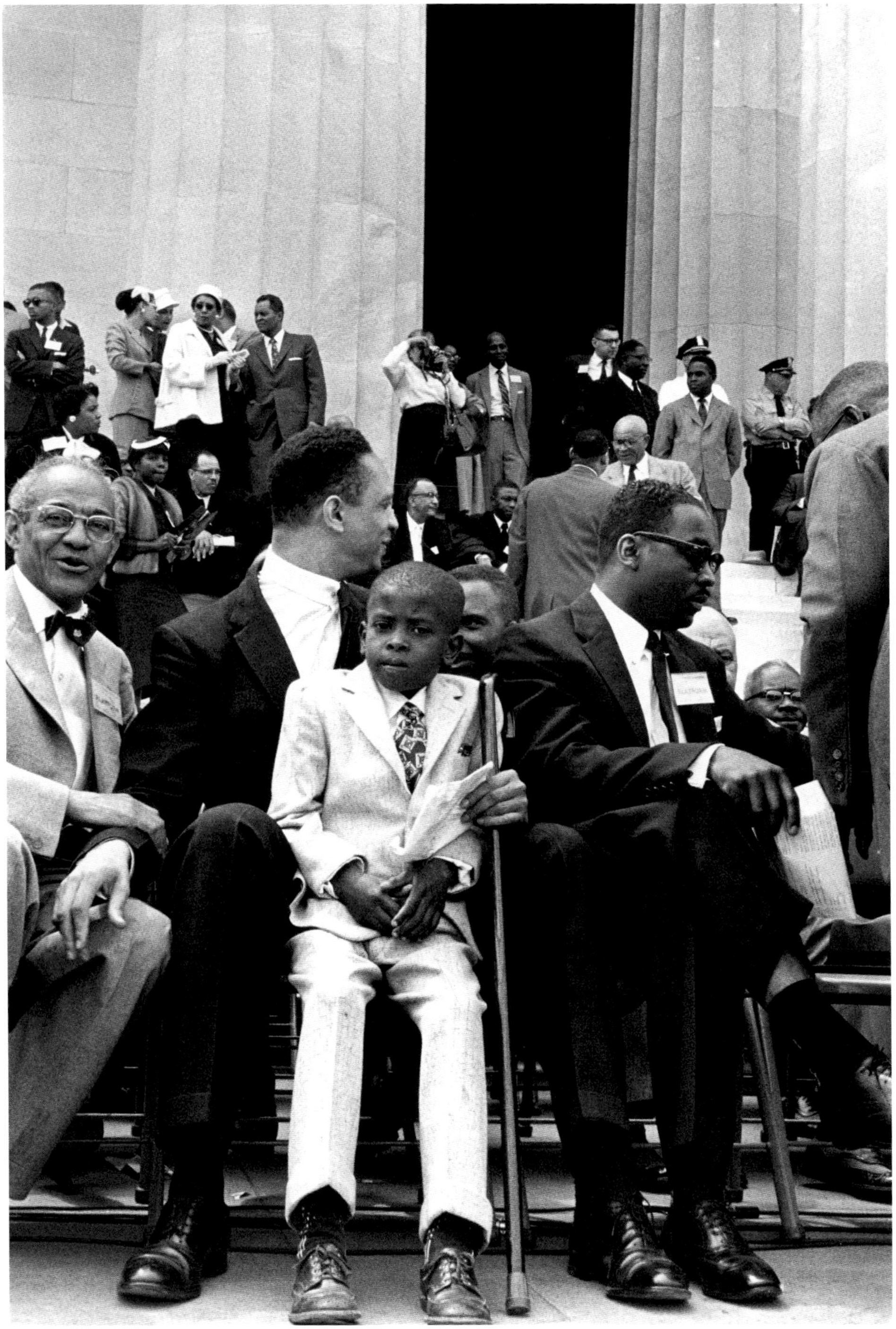

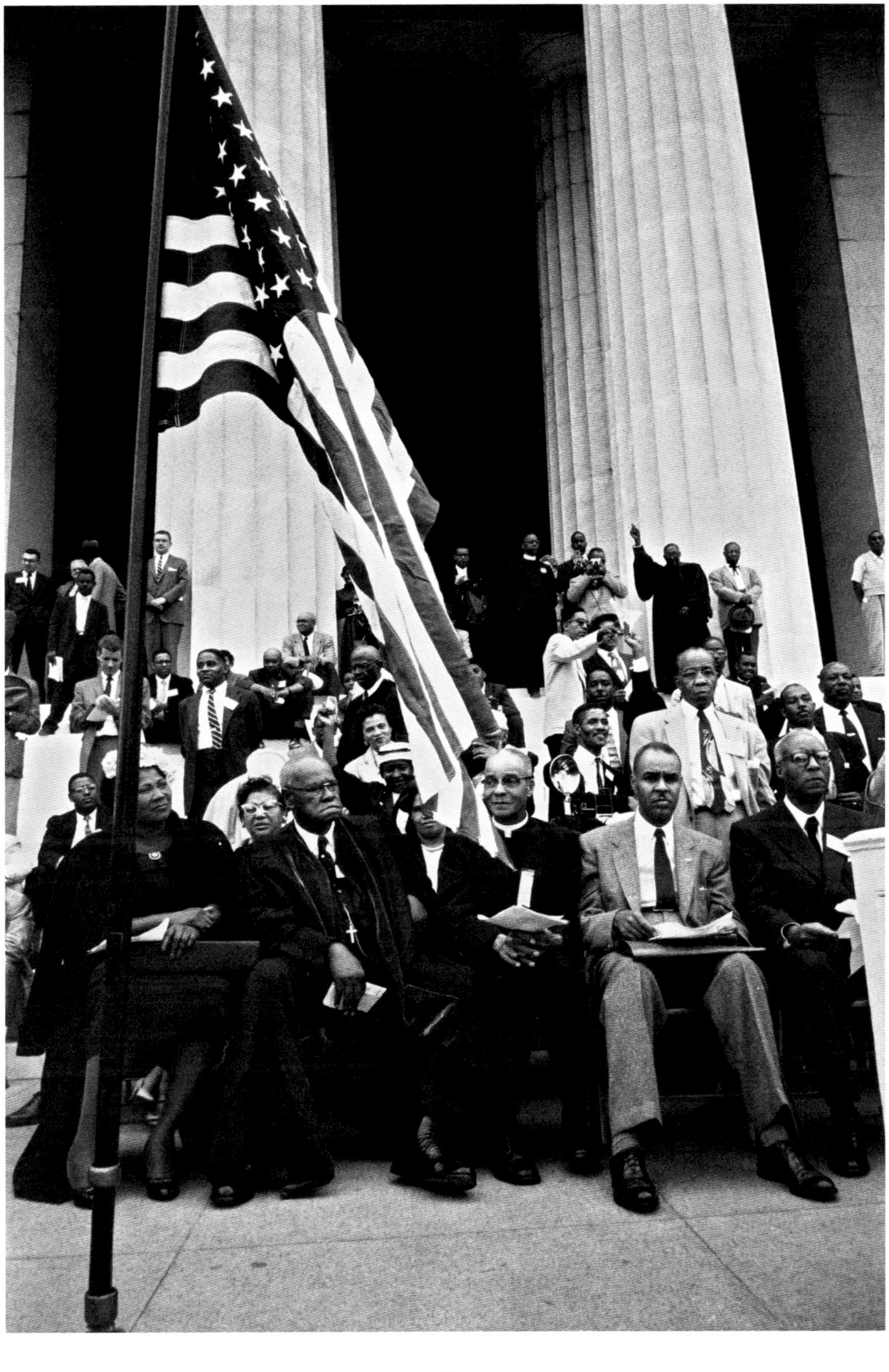

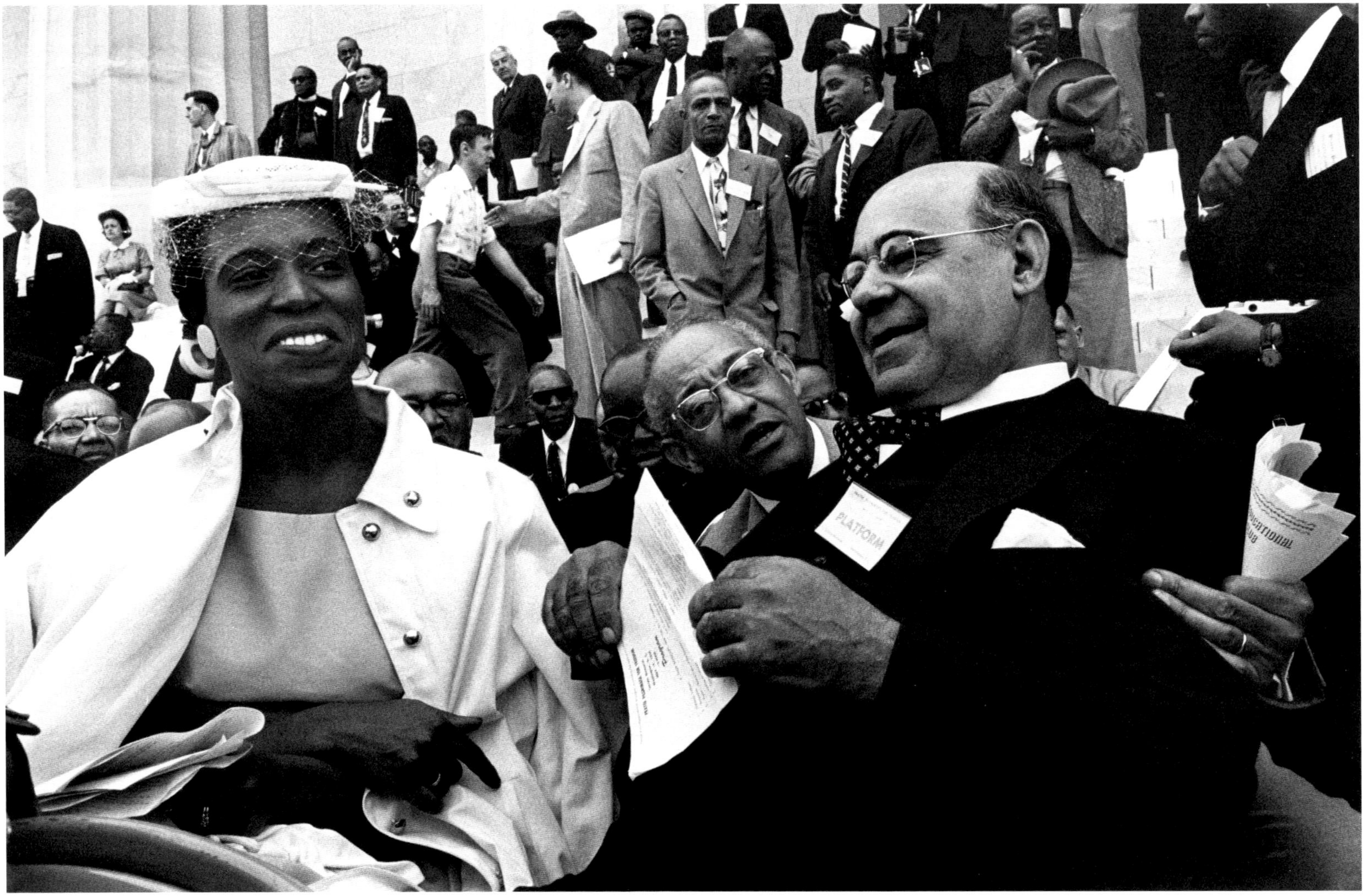
PLATFORM

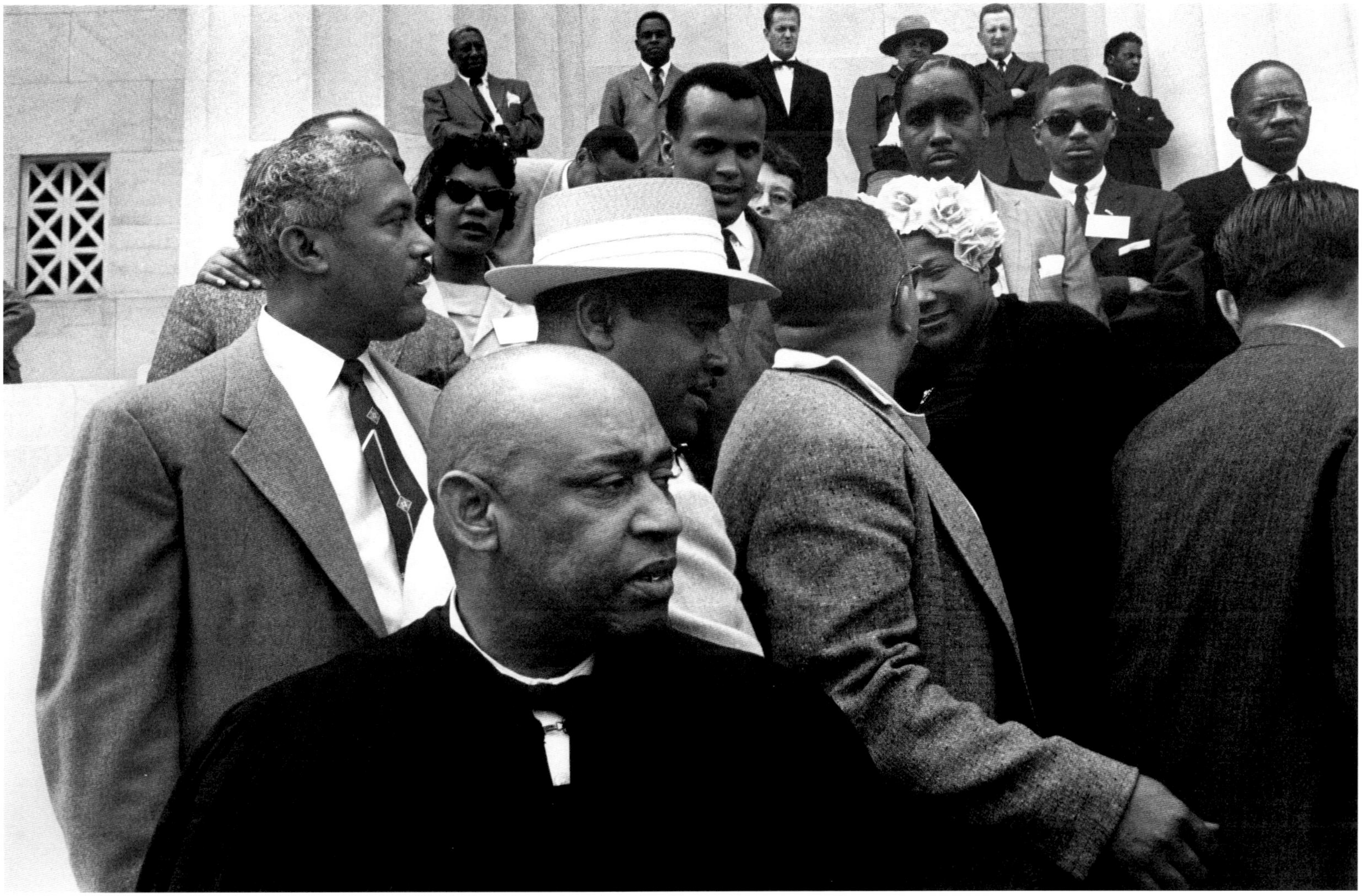

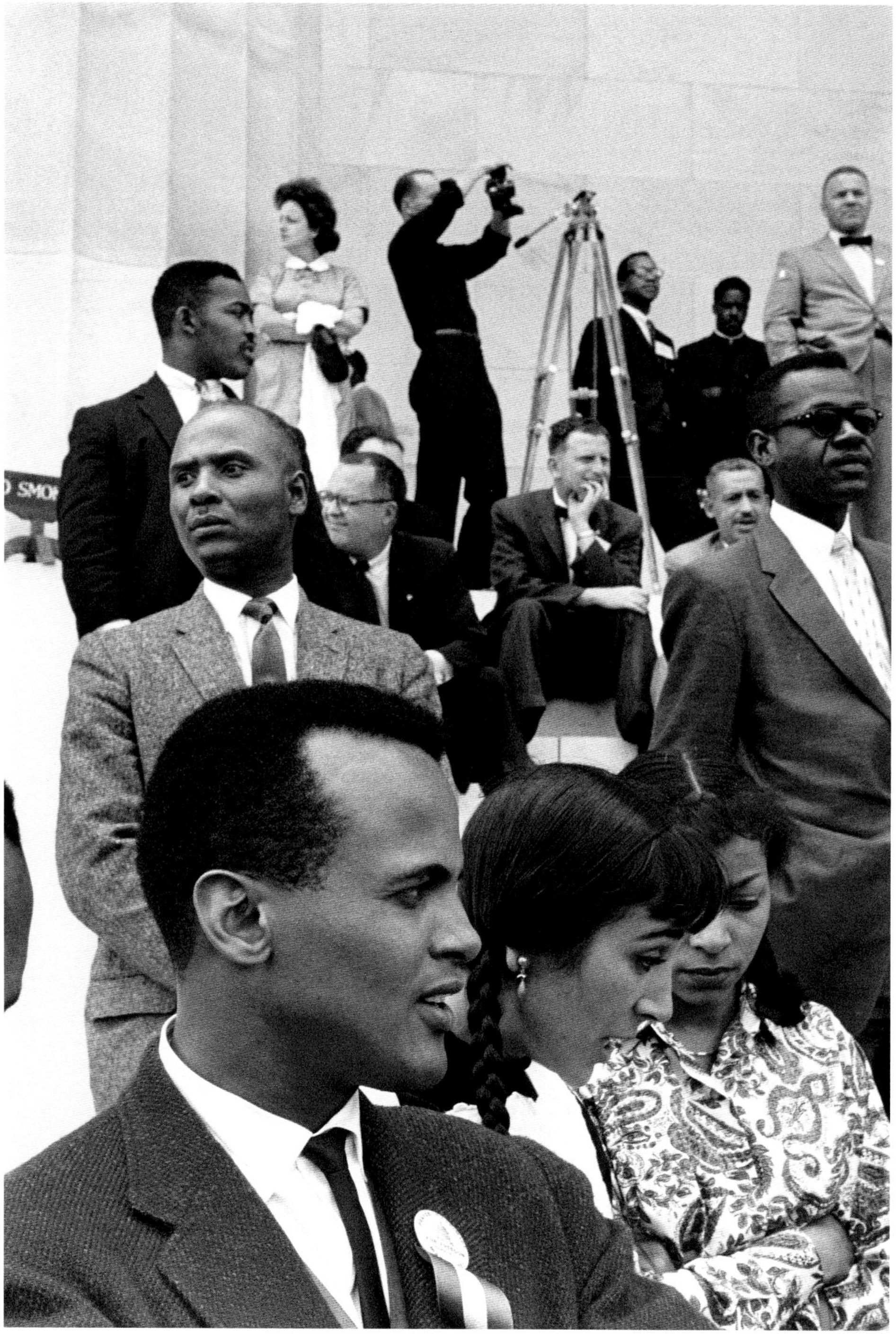

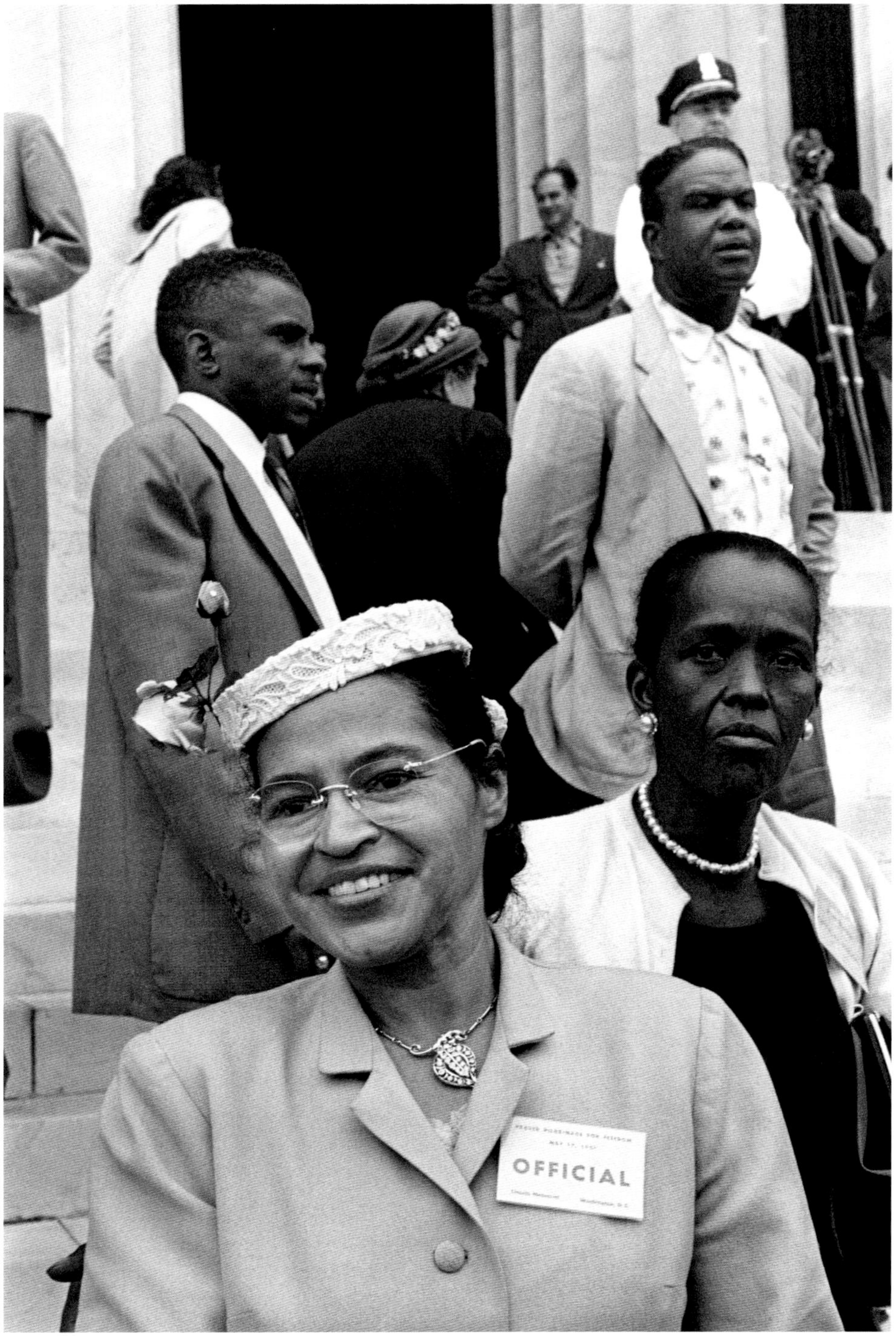
OFFICIAL

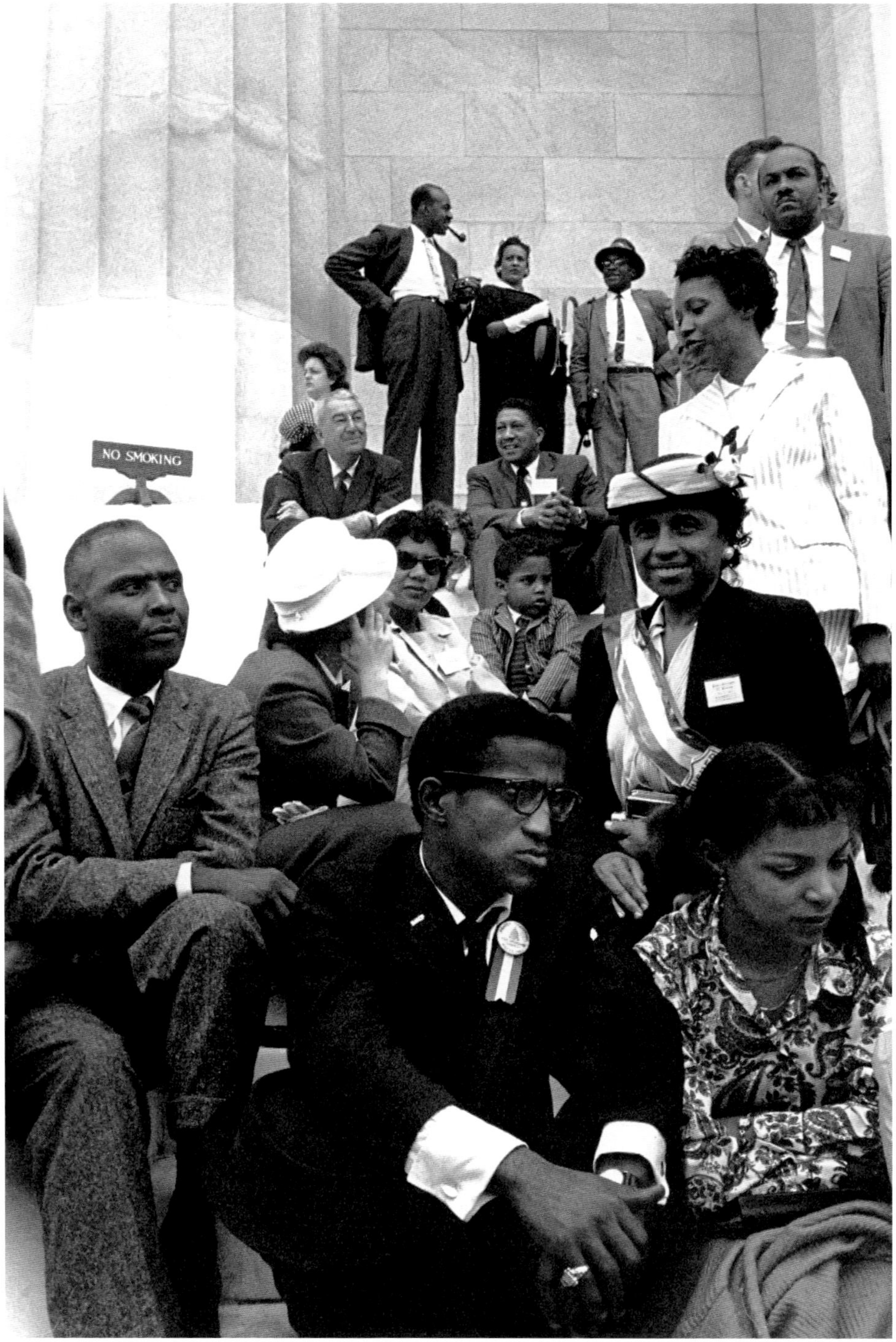
NO SMOKING

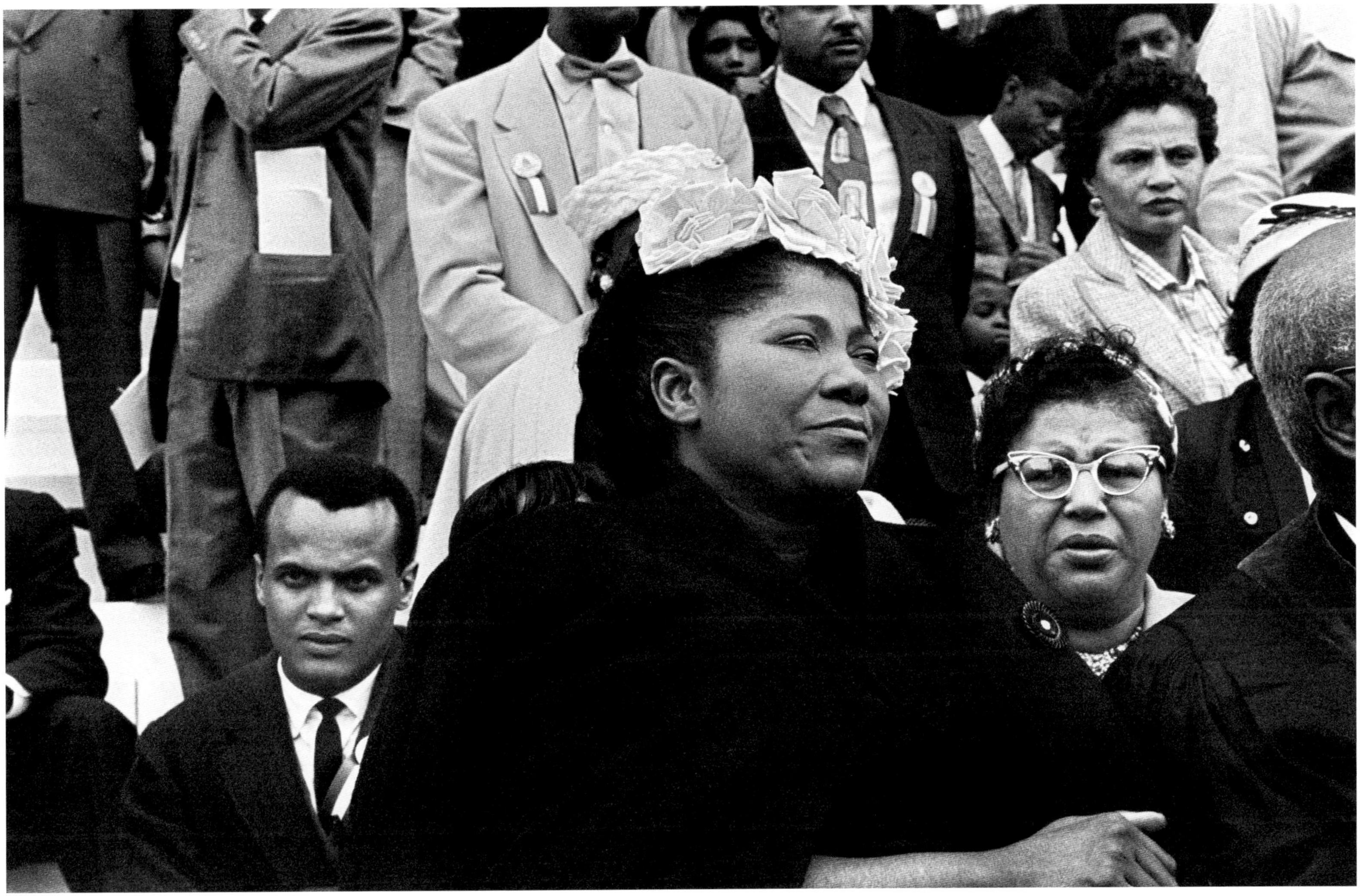

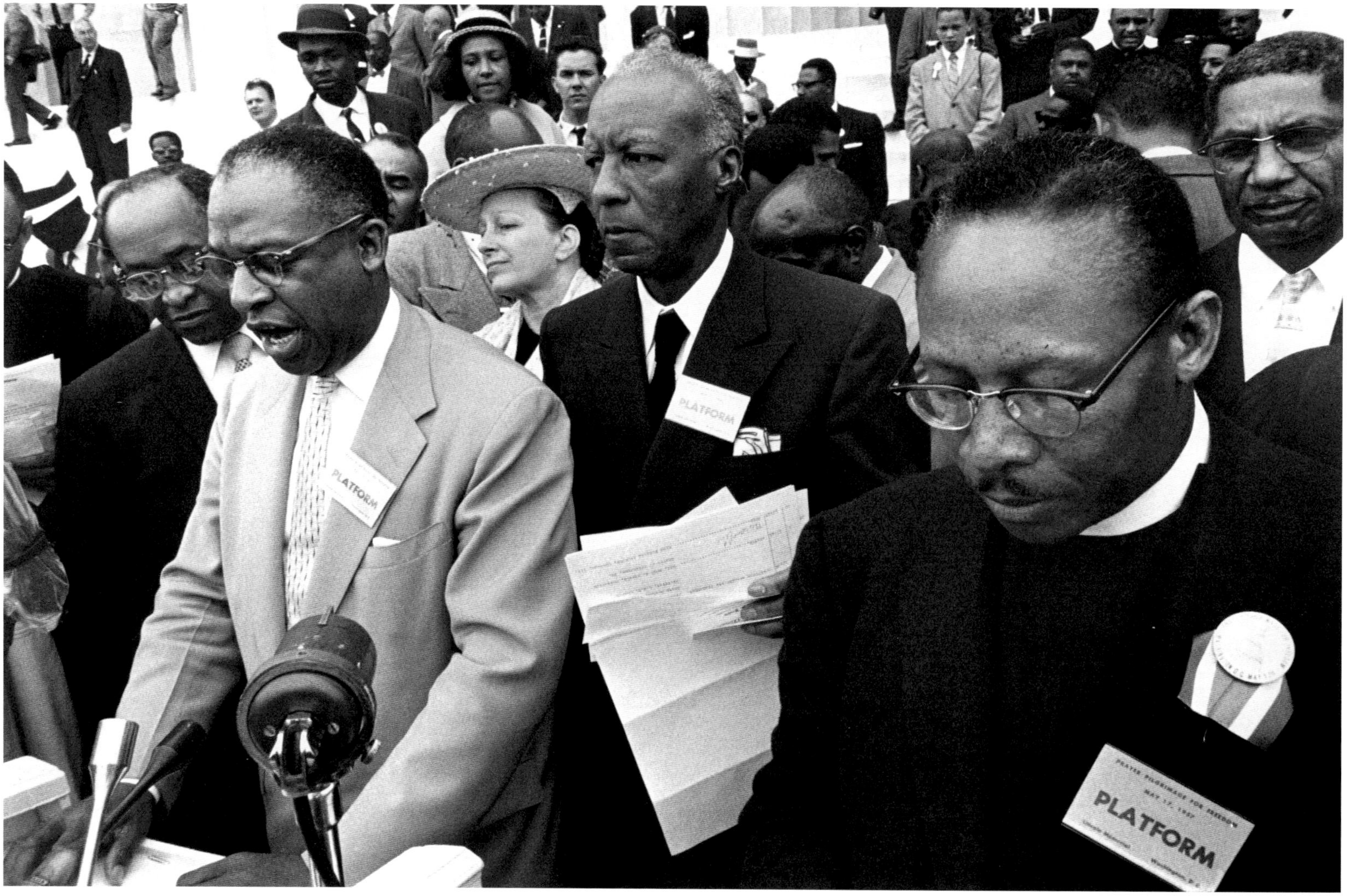
PLATFORM
PLATFORM
PLATFORM

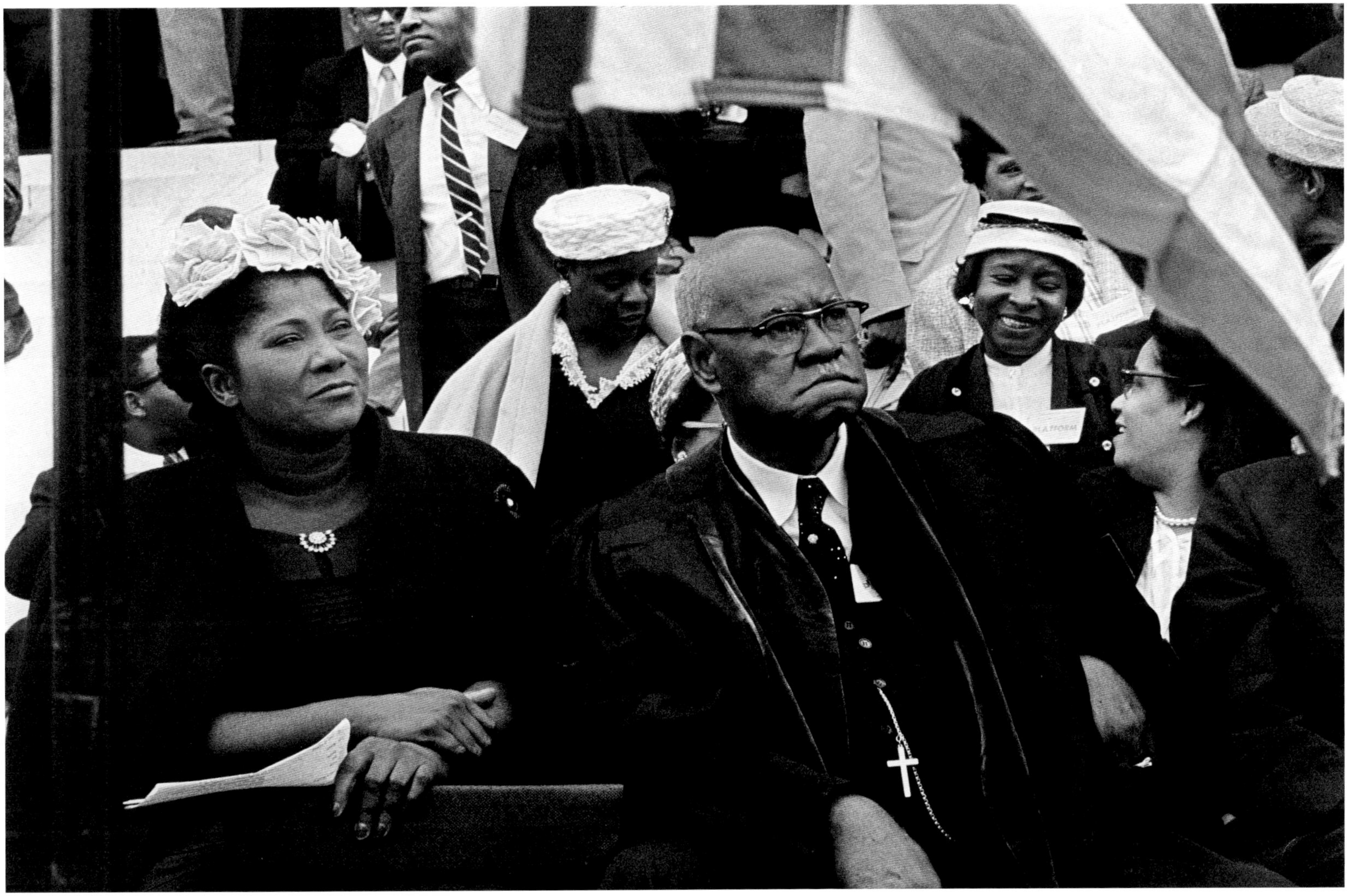

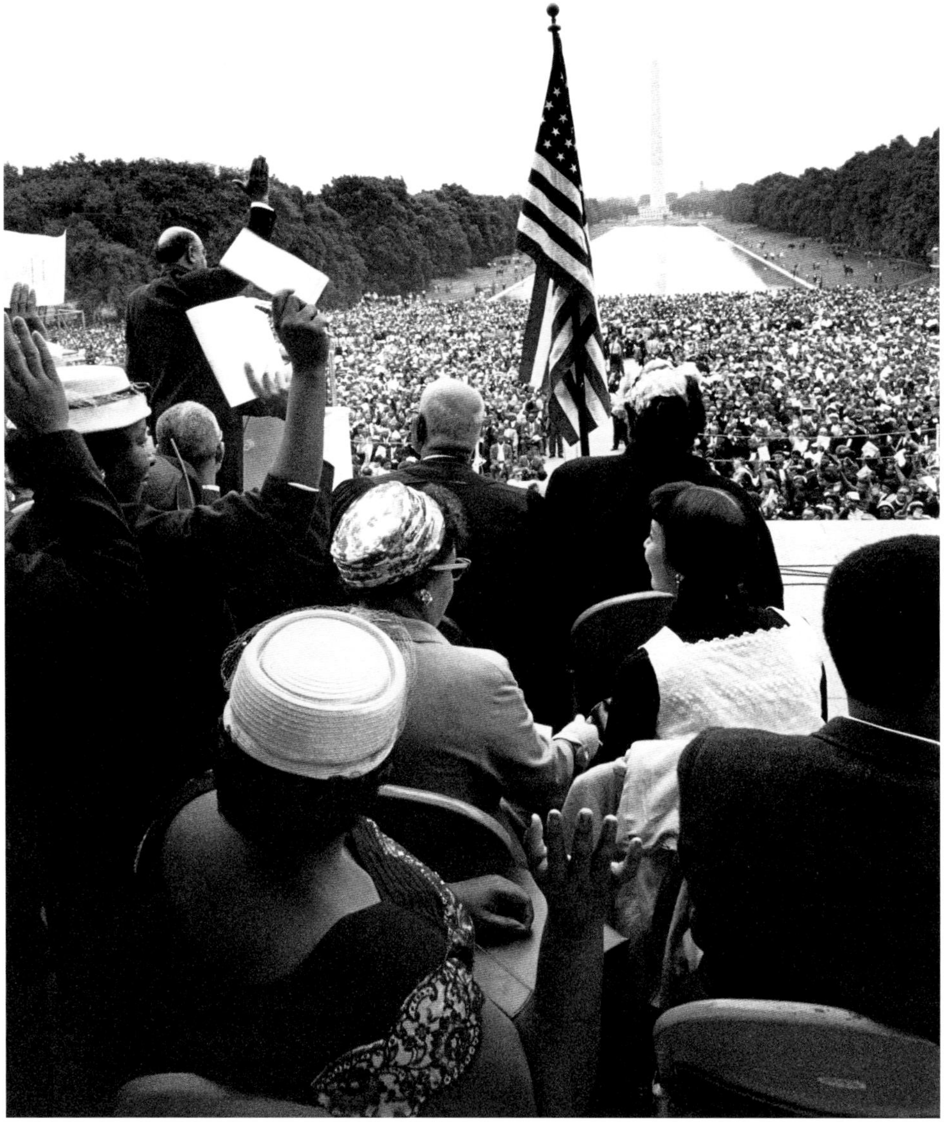

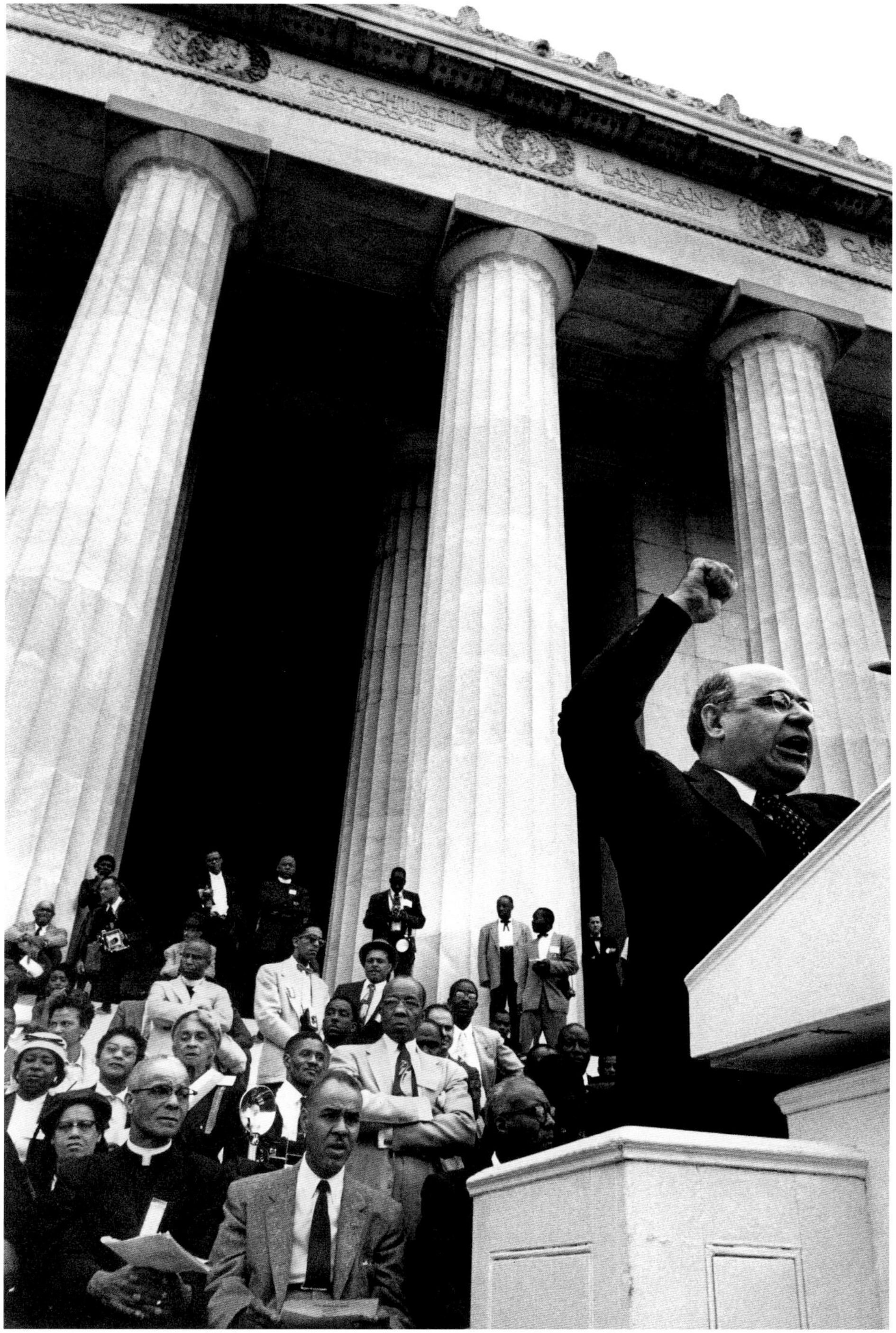
MASSACHUSETTS
MARYLAND

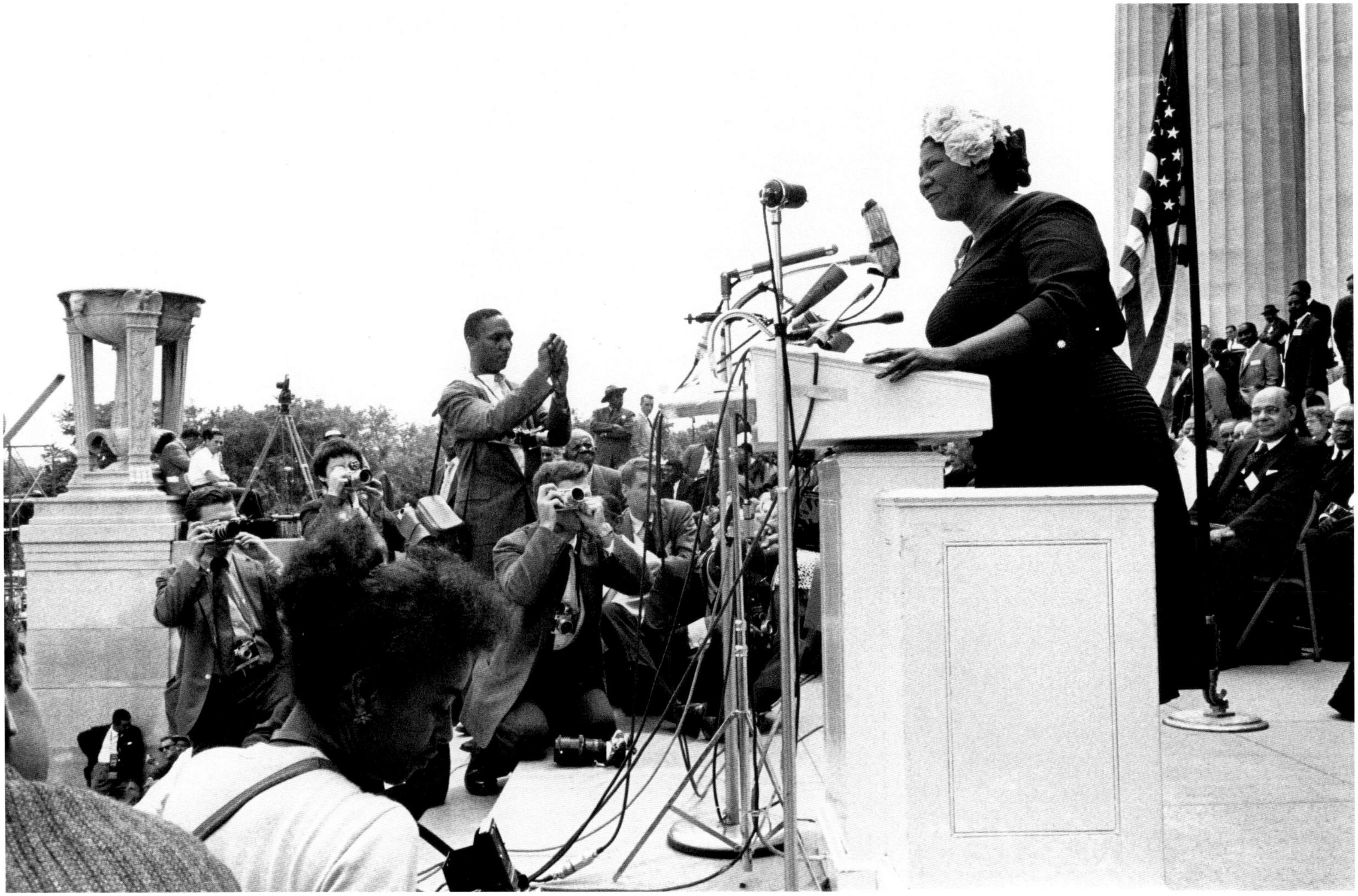

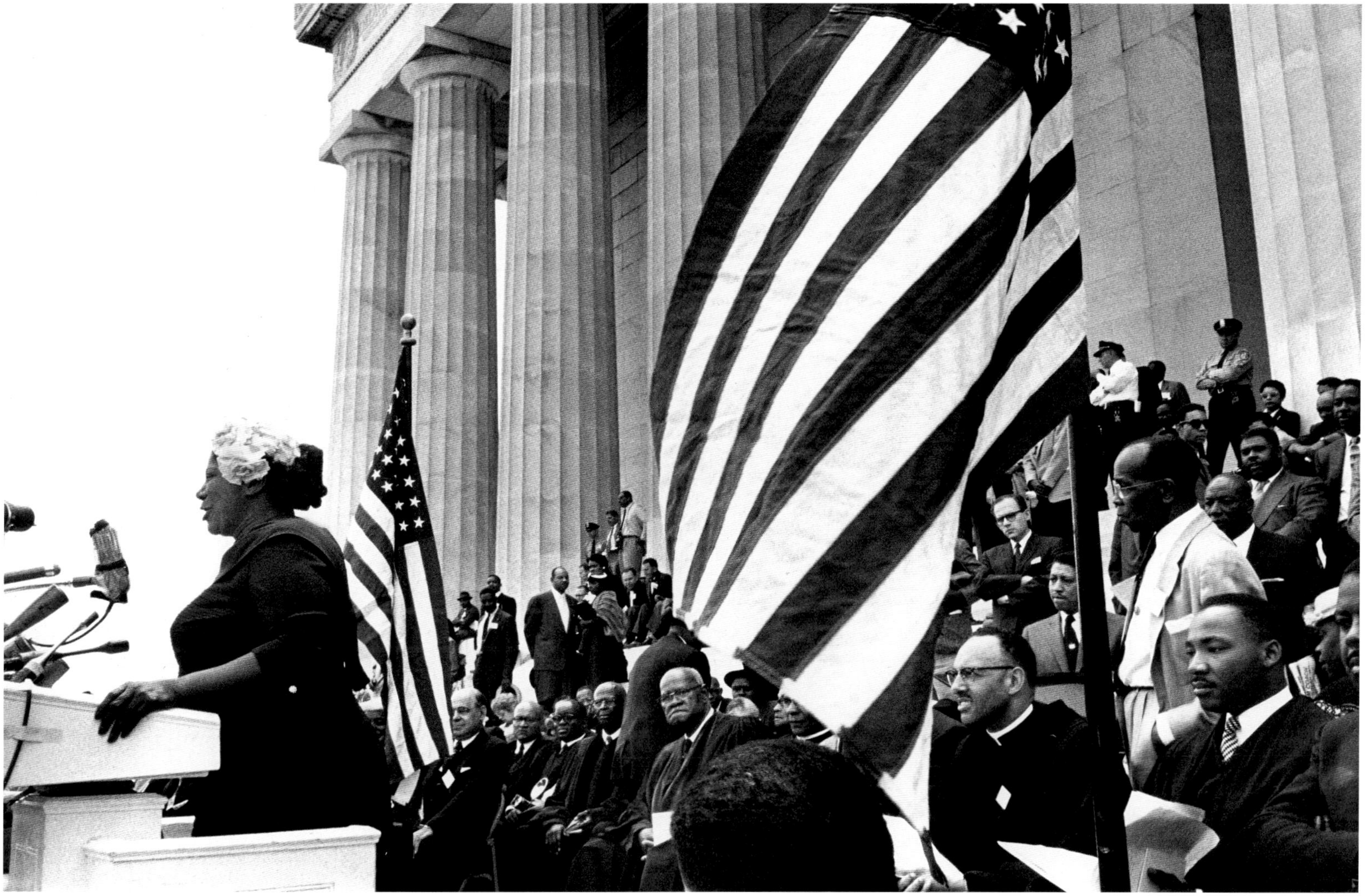

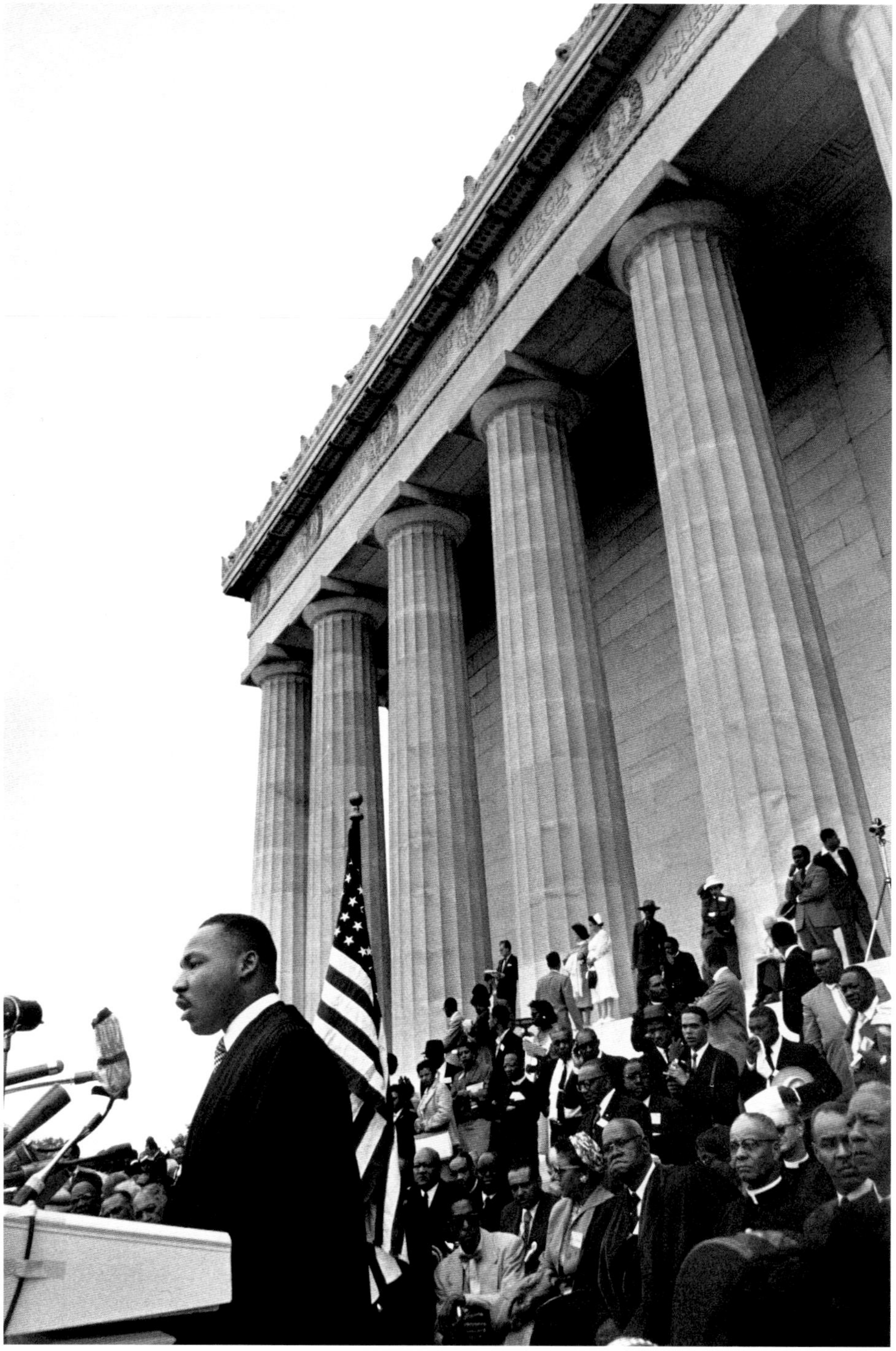
GEORGIA

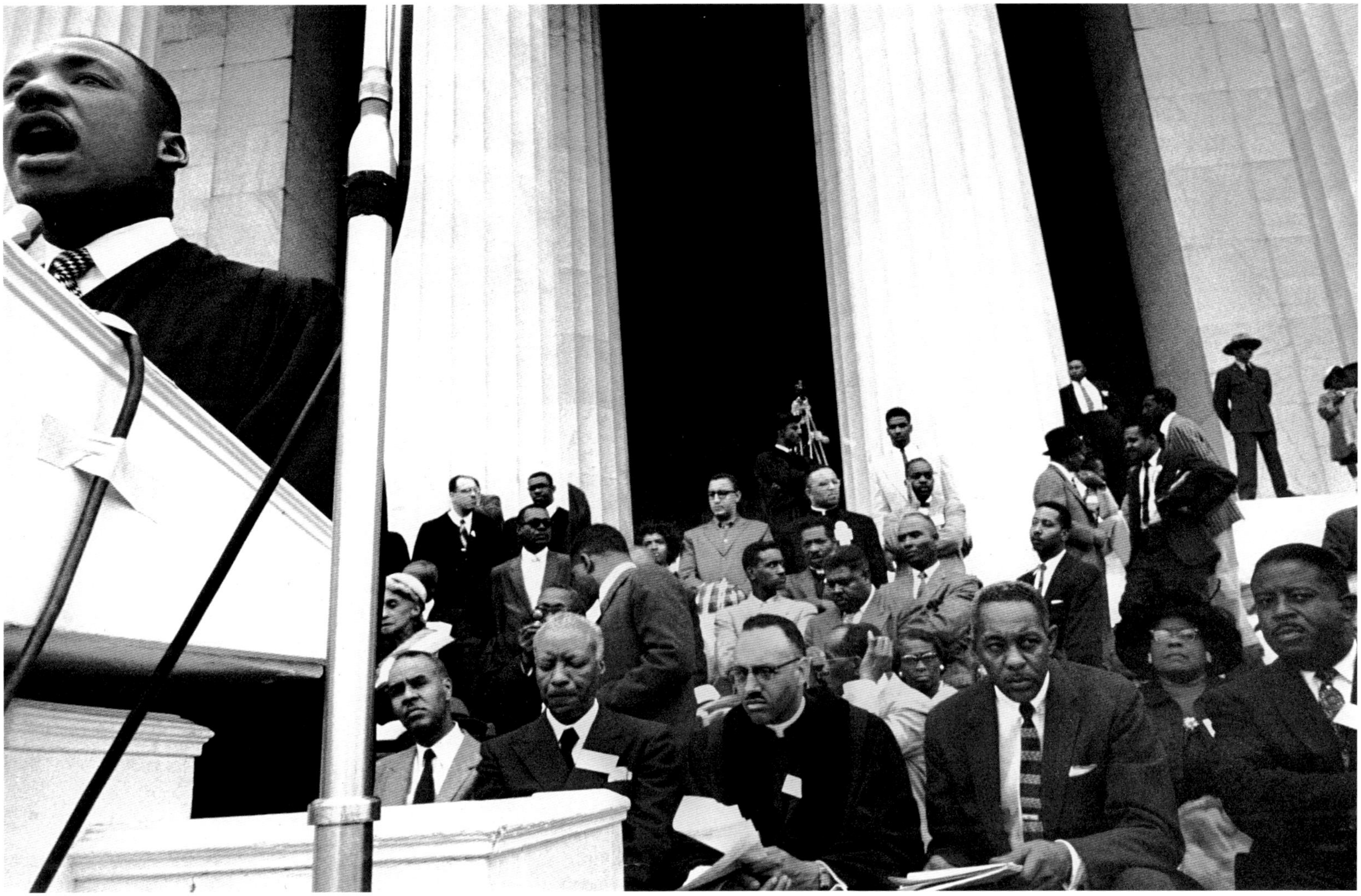

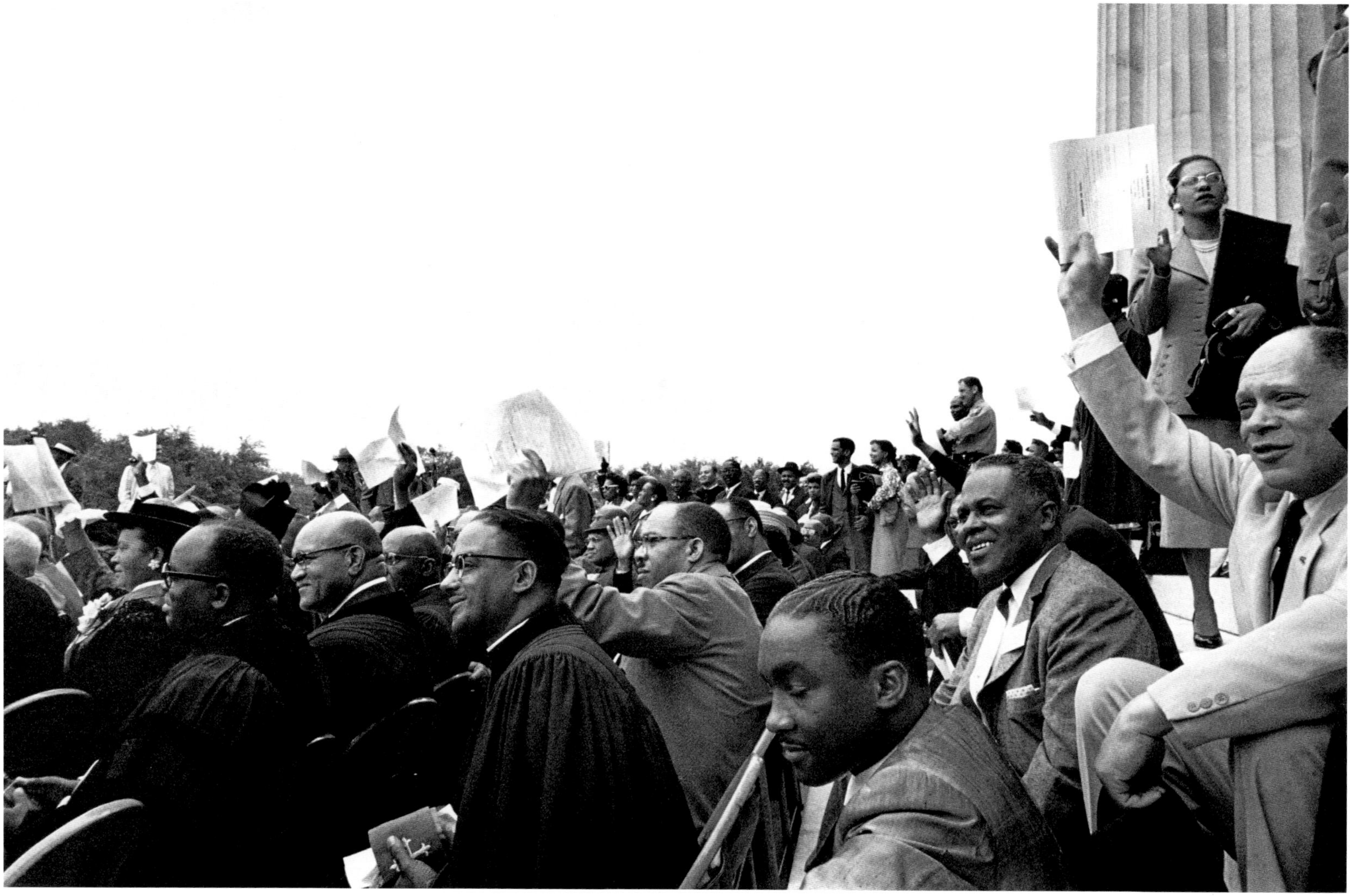

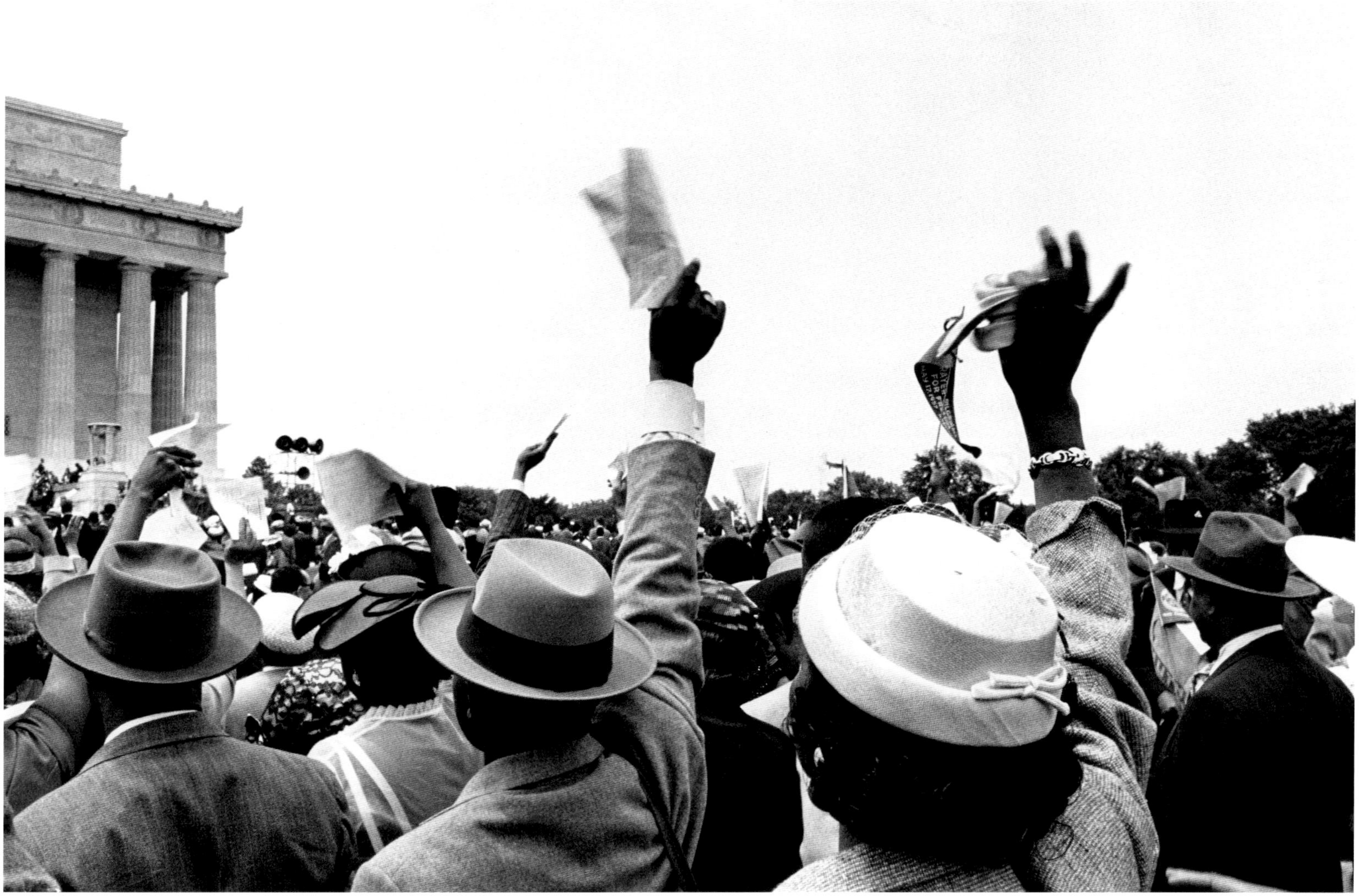

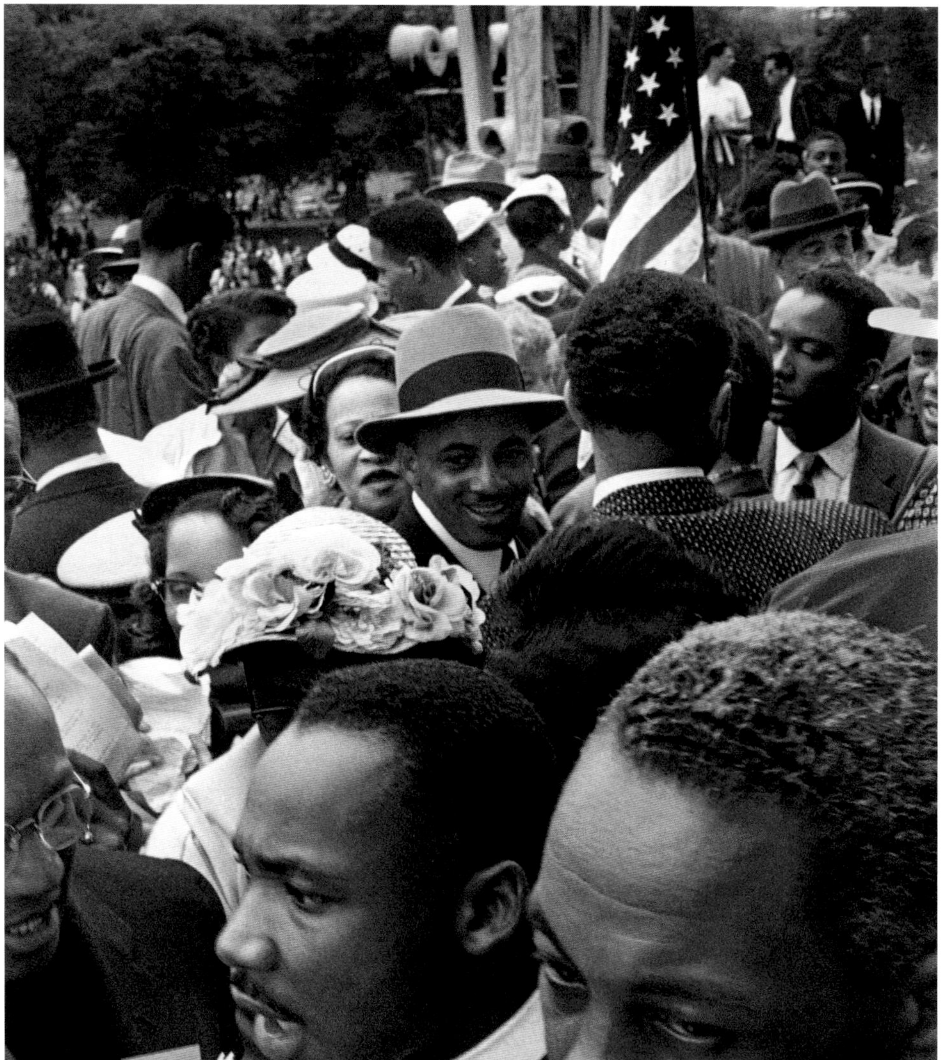

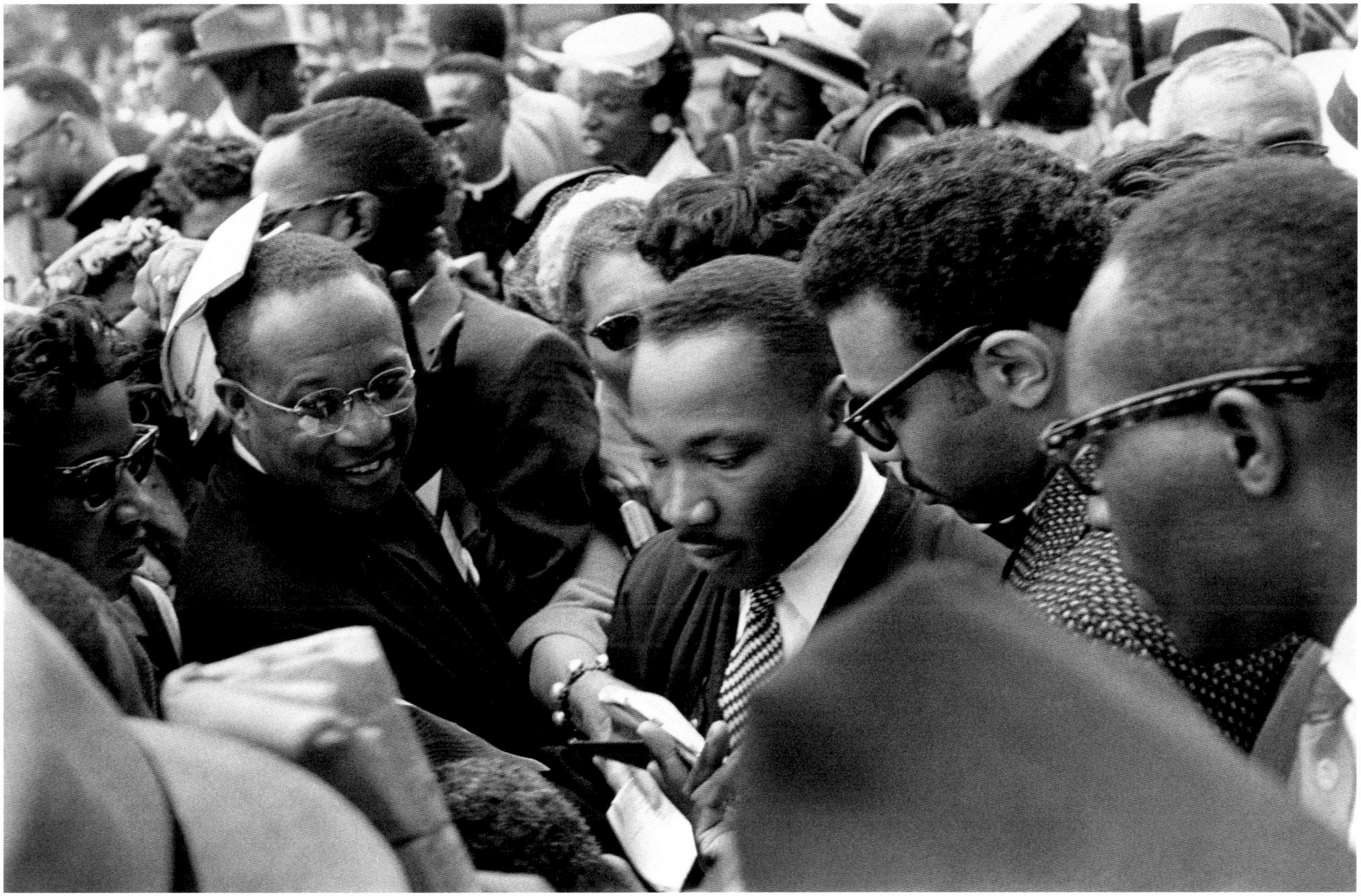

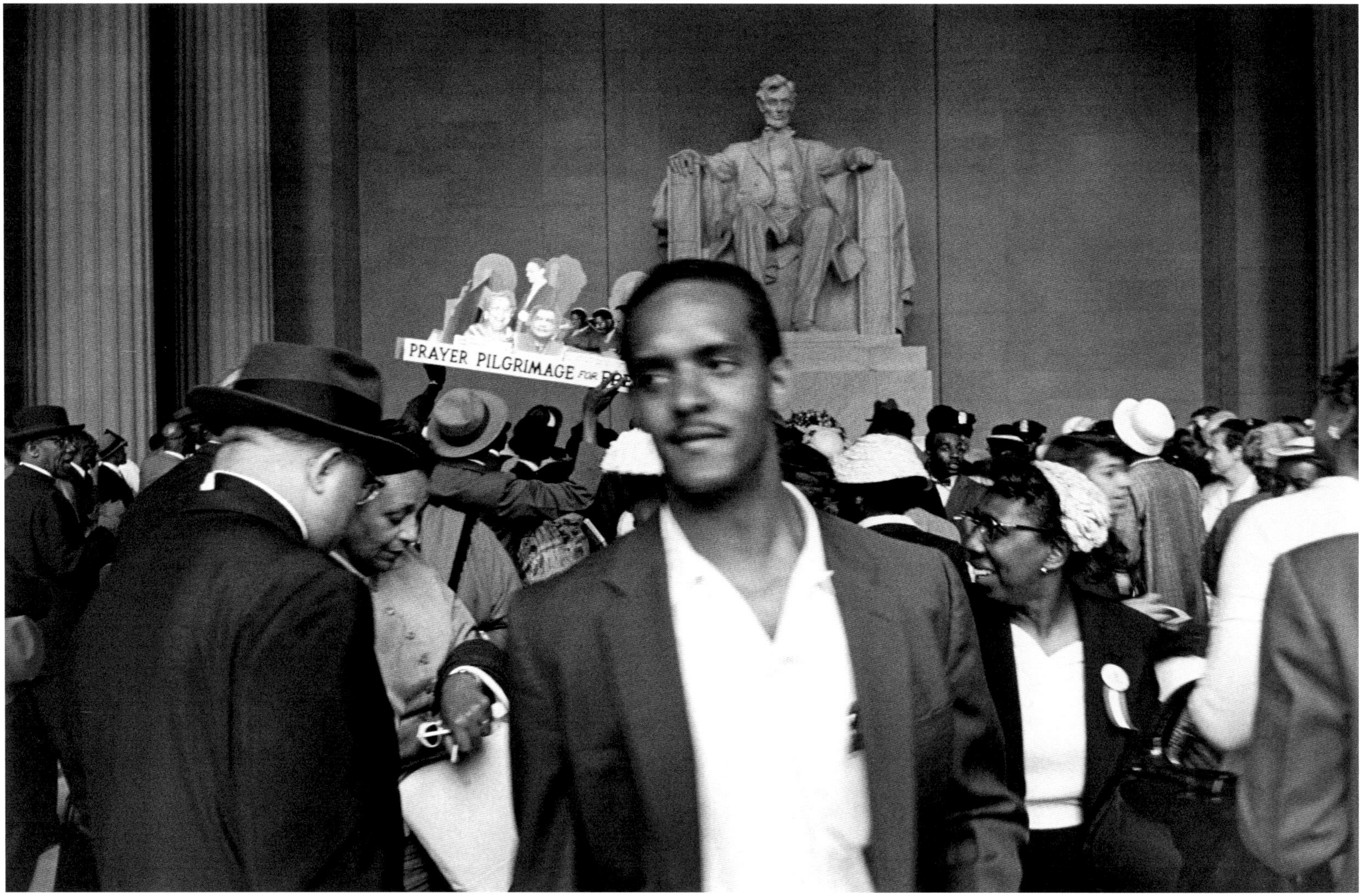
PRAYER PILGRIMAGE FOR

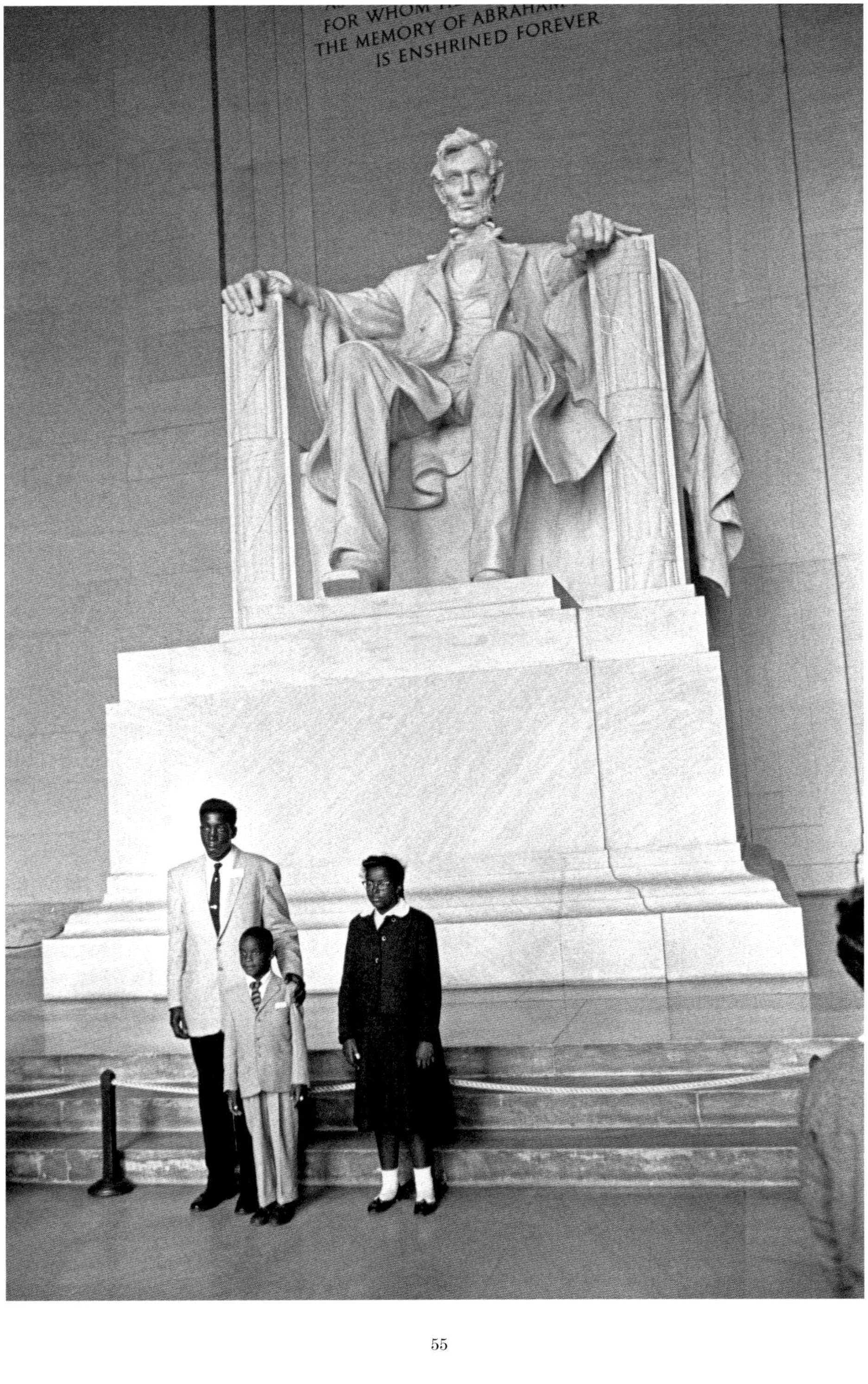
FOR WHOM
THE MEMORY OF ABRAHAM
IS ENSHRINED FOREVER

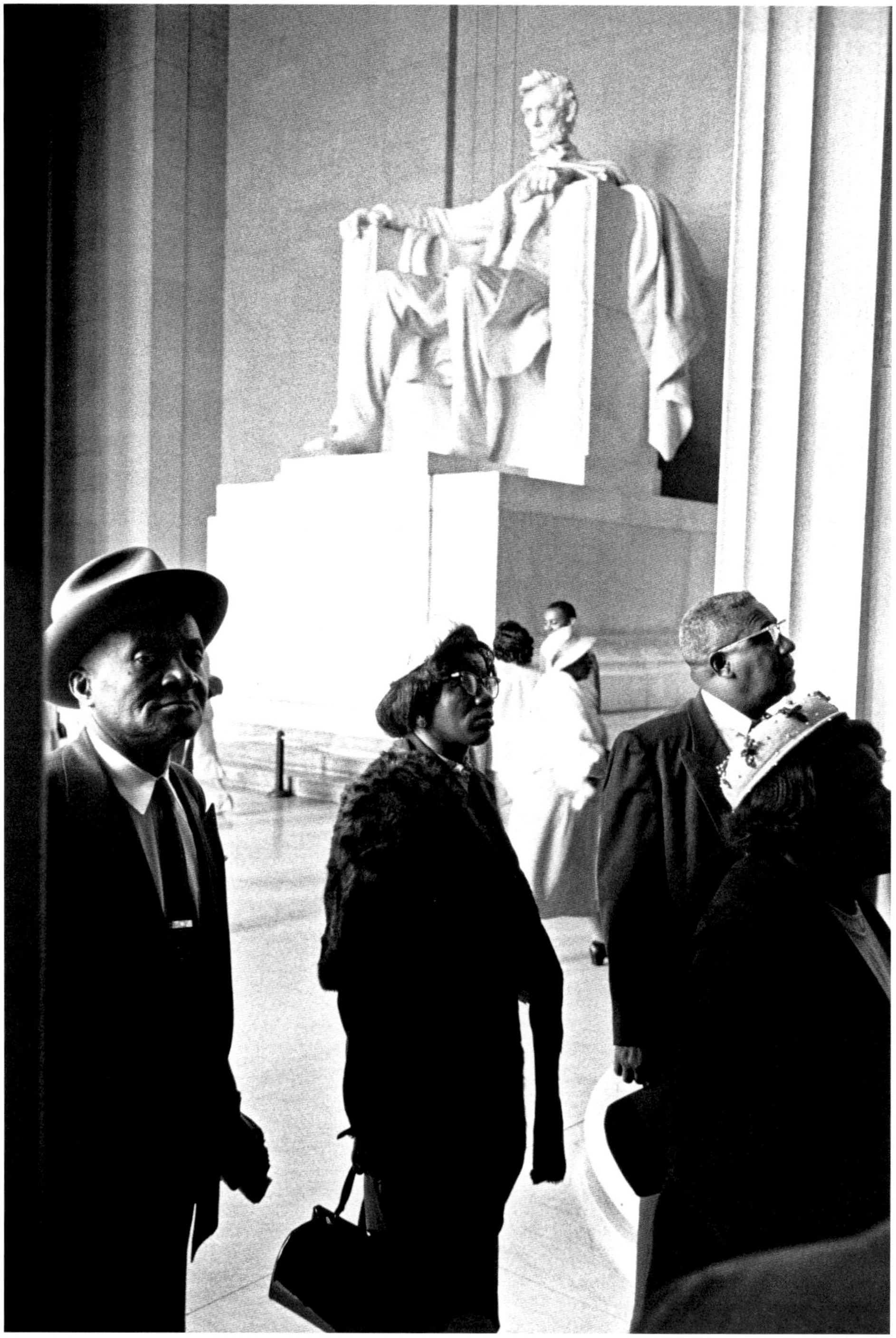

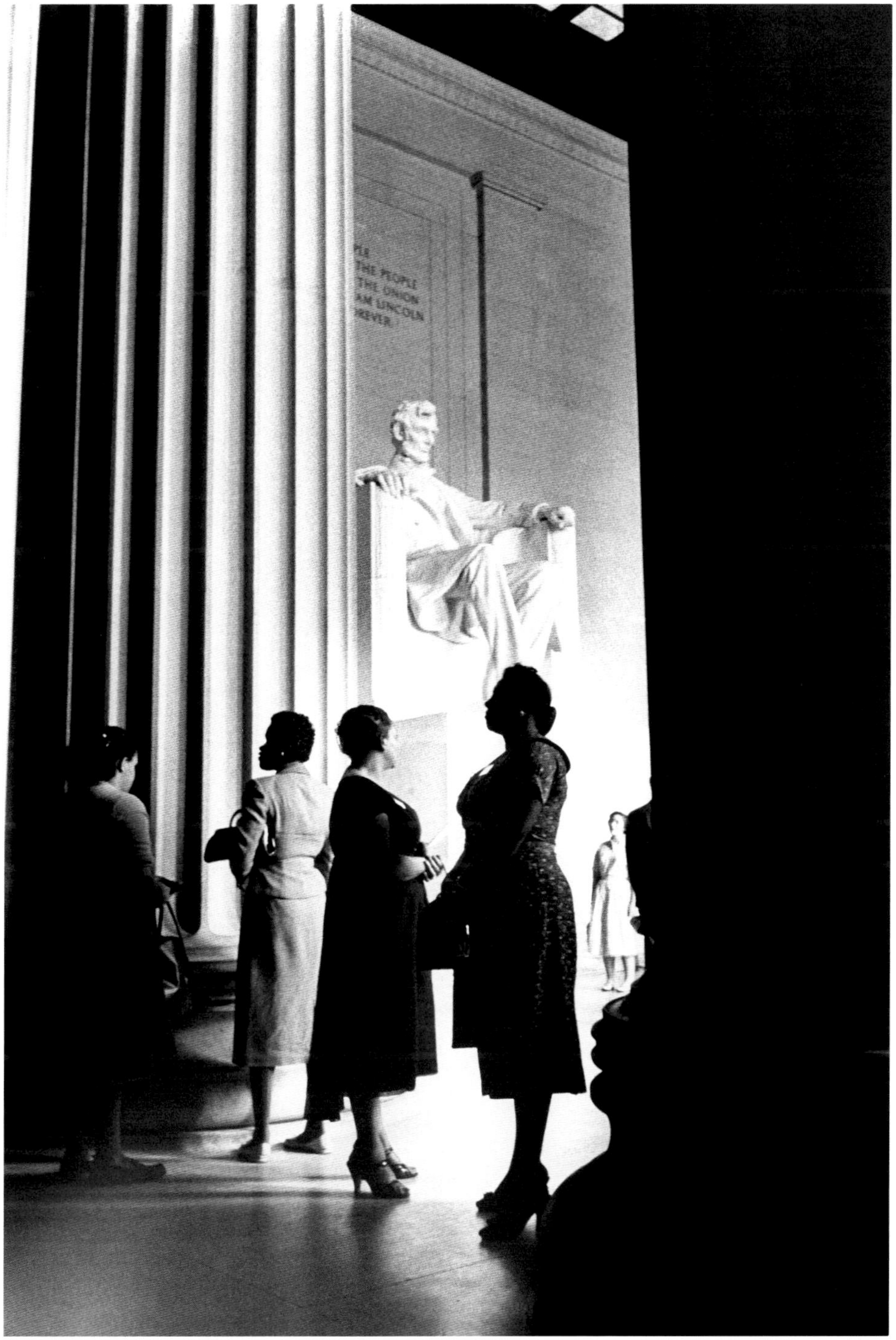
THE PEOPLE
THE UNION
AM LINCOLN

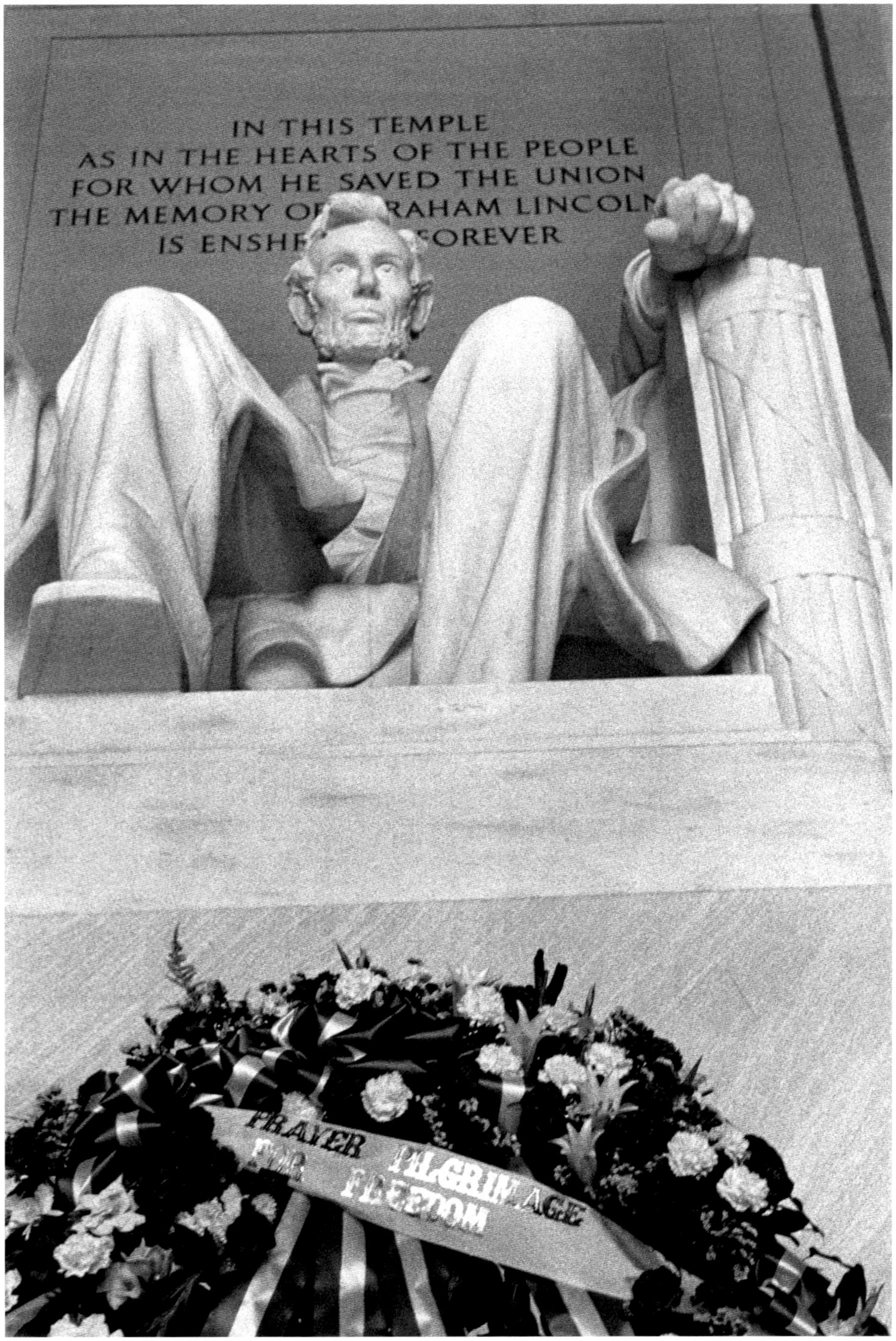
IN THIS TEMPLE
AS IN THE HEARTS OF THE PEOPLE
FOR WHOM HE SAVED THE UNION
PRAYER PILGRIMAGE
FREEDOM

CAPTIONS

Captions are provided for photographs in which subjects have been identified and confirmed.

plate 34: Bishop William Yancey Bell (left) and Lewis E. Martin (center)

35: First row: Mahalia Jackson, Bishop Sherman Lawrence Greene, Bishop William Jacob Walls, Roy Wilkins, and A. Philip Randolph; Jesse M. Tinsley (second row standing)

36: Rose Battle English, Bishop William Yancey Bell, and Mordecai Johnson

37: Background: Harry Belafonte and Mahalia Jackson

38: Harry Belafonte, Julie Belafonte, and Ruby Dee

39: Rosa Parks and Ella Baker

40: Front: Sammy Davis, Jr. and Ruby Dee; Eugene T. Reed (background seated)

41: Harry Belafonte and Mahalia Jackson

42: A. Philip Randolph (center) and Reverend Thomas J. Kilgore, Jr. (right)

43: Mahalia Jackson and Bishop Sherman Lawrence Greene

44: Mordecai Johnson (at podium)

45: Mordecai Johnson (at podium); first row: Bishop William Jacob Walls, Roy Wilkins, and A. Philip Randolph; Jesse M. Tinsley (second row standing)

46: Mahalia Jackson (at podium); first row: Mordecai Johnson

47: Mahalia Jackson (at podium); first row: Mordecai Johnson, Bishop Sherman Lawrence Greene, Reverend Thomas J. Kilgore, Jr. and Reverend Martin Luther King, Jr.

48: Reverend Martin Luther King, Jr. (at podium); first row: Bishop Sherman Lawrence Greene, Bishop William Jacob Walls, Roy Wilkins and A. Philip Randolph

49: Reverend Martin Luther King, Jr. (at podium); first row: Roy Wilkins, A. Philip Randolph, Reverend Thomas J. Kilgore, Jr., unknown, and Ralph Abernathy; Vivian Carter Mason (second row right)

50: Edward Turner (far right)

52: Elmer Carter and Reverend Martin Luther King, Jr.

53: Elmer Carter and Reverend Martin Luther King, Jr.

Because of the religious nature of this program, we are asking that applause be withheld.

PRAYER PILGRIMAGE FOR FREEDOM

Lincoln Memorial

Washington, D. C.

MAY 17, 1957

12 NOON

Program

A. PHILIP RANDOLPH, New York, N. Y., *Presiding*

1. National Anthem	Led by MISS ROSE BATTLE ENGLISH, New York, N. Y.
2. Invocation	BISHOP S. L. GREENE, Atlanta, Ga., Senior Bishop, AME Church
3. Hymn — Battle Hymn of the Republic	CHORUS, Directed by PROF. WARNER LAWSON, Washington, D. C.
4. Laying of Wreath	JAMES and THERESA GORDON, Formerly of Clay, Ky.
5. Opening Remarks	Co-Chairman A. PHILIP RANDOLPH, New York, N. Y., International President, Brotherhood of Sleeping Car Porters, AFL-CIO
6. Hymn — A Mighty Fortress Is Our God	CHORUS
7. Scripture Reading — Old Testament	BISHOP WILLIAM J. WALLS, Chicago, Ill., Senior Bishop, AMEZ Church
8. Scripture Reading — New Testament	BISHOP WILLIAM Y. BELL, South Boston, Va. Third Episcopal District, CME Church
9. Prayer	REV. ROSS A. WESTON, Unitarian Church of Arlington, Va.
10. Solo	MISS MAHALIA JACKSON, Chicago, Ill.
11. Remarks	MRS. IRENE McCOY GAINES, Chicago, Ill., President, National Association of Colored Women
12. Remarks	MRS. WILLIAM T. MASON, Norfolk, Va., President, National Council of Negro Women
13. Litany of Freedom (Turn over for words)	Led by REV. THOMAS J. KILGORE, JR., Friendship Baptist Church, New York, N. Y.
14. Remarks	DR. MORDECAI W. JOHNSON, President, Howard University, Washington, D. C.
15. Spiritual	CHORUS AND AUDIENCE
16. Reports of Southern Freedom Fighters	REV. WILLIAM H. BORDERS, Atlanta, Ga., Wheat Street Baptist Church
	REV. C. K. STEELE, Tallahassee, Fla., Bethel Baptist Church
	REV. F. L. SHUTTLESWORTH, Birmingham, Ala., Bethel Baptist Church
	REV. A. L. DAVIS, New Orleans, La., New Zion Baptist Church
17. Anthem — Lift Ev'ry Voice and Sing (Turn over for words)	CHORUS AND AUDIENCE
18. Prayer	DR. NORMAN GERSTENFELD, Rabbi, Washington Hebrew Congregation
19. Remarks	Co-Chairman ROY WILKINS, Executive Secretary, NAACP, New York, N. Y.
20. Scripture Reading	DR. W. H. JERNAGIN, Washington, D. C., Chairman, Executive Committee, Fraternal Council of Negro Churches
21. Solo	MISS MAHALIA JACKSON, Chicago, Ill.
22. Scripture Reading	BISHOP R. C. LAWSON, New York, N. Y., Refuge Temple
23. Remarks	HON. PAUL H. DOUGLAS, U. S. Senator from Illinois
24. Remarks	HON. CHARLES C. DIGGS, JR., Representative, 13th District, Michigan
25. Remarks	HON. JACOB K. JAVITS, U. S. Senator from New York
26. Remarks	HON. ADAM CLAYTON POWELL, Representative, 16th District, New York
27. Music	PHILADELPHIA FELLOWSHIP HOUSE CHOIR, MRS. AILEEN BROWN, Director
28. Remarks	REV. MARTIN LUTHER KING, Co-Chairman, Montgomery, Ala., Dexter Avenue Baptist Church
29. Affirmation and Pledge	
30. My Country 'Tis of Thee	CHORUS AND AUDIENCE
31. Benediction	REV. T. M. CHAMBERS, Los Angeles, Calif., Zion Hill Baptist Church

A LITANY OF FREEDOM

LEADER: It is a good thing to gather in this hallowed place to give thanks unto the Lord, and to sing praises unto the name of the Most High. It is our will and desire that men pray everywhere, lifting up hands unto God without wrath and malice.

LEADER & MINISTERS: Lift up your hearts.

PEOPLE: We lift them up unto the Lord.

LEADER & MINISTERS: Almighty God, the Father of all mankind, hear us while we pray: Forgive us of our sins and purge our lives with the purity of Thy love.

PEOPLE: We beseech Thee to hear us, O God.

LEADER & MINISTERS: Bless all people everywhere, and so turn the hearts of men toward each other that inequalities and injustices may disappear and the spirit of brotherhood may dwell among us.

PEOPLE: We beseech Thee to hear us, O God.

LEADER & MINISTERS: Grant unto us the will and the spirit to keep faith in our country. Give us the forgiving spirit that will enable us to love those who would destroy our heritage of freedom, and give us the courage to press ever forward for full freedom for all Thy children.

PEOPLE: We beseech Thee to hear us, O God.

LEADER & MINISTERS: Grant that we may never betray the martyrs who have suffered for freedom, for good government, for just laws, for the sanctity of the home, for fair returns for labor given and for the right to live freely and unmolested.

PEOPLE: We beseech Thee to hear us, O God.

LEADER & MINISTERS: Grant that the leaders of the world may be conscious of the greatness of their tasks. Arouse the Conscience of the leaders of our country. Give unto them a sense of honor, let their workmanship be conscientious and thorough. Rid them of petty selfishness, blind prejudice, bigoted avarice and political dishonesty.

PEOPLE: We humbly beseech Thee to hear us, O God.

LEADER & MINISTERS: Bless the pilgrims who have come from far and near, let each one be fired inwardly to work and sacrifice for peace and freedom.

PEOPLE: We beseech Thee to hear us, O God.

COLLECT

LEADER, MINISTERS & PEOPLE:

Grant unto us, O Lord, a sufficiency of Thy grace that we may do justly, love mercy and walk humbly with Thee. So order our lives that justice will run down like waters and righteousness as a mighty stream. So lead us in the future that we may find the Way, the Truth and the Life, and so be free by the discovery of Truth, through Jesus Christ Our Lord, Amen.

LIFT EV'RY VOICE AND SING

Lift ev'ry voice and sing
Till earth and heaven ring,
Ring with the harmonies of Liberty;
Let our rejoicing rise
High as the list'ning skies,
Let it resound loud as the rolling sea.
Sing a song full of the faith that the dark past has taught us,
Sing a song full of the hope that the present has brought us,
Facing the rising sun of our new day begun,
Let us march on till victory is won.

AFFIRMATION AND PLEDGE

We believe in the fatherhood of God and the brotherhood of all mankind.

We believe that democracy is the noblest political expression of this religious faith.

We believe that in the household of God there can be no discrimination among his children on the irrelevant basis of race, color or religious affiliation.

We believe that to compel the segregation of the children of God on such basis is sinful defiance of God's will.

We believe that the American people of whatever racial origin or of whatever church affiliation are deeply religious and wish to order their lives and their country according to the great moral truths of our common religious heritage and the inspiring principles of our democratic society.

In this conviction we call upon all Americans to join us in prayer and in work to eradicate racial and religious prejudices so that every American may freely enjoy the fruits of our common efforts to advance humanity.

We believe firmly in the ultimate triumph of this faith in the fatherhood of God and the brotherhood of man.

426

Call to a PRAYER PILGRIMAGE *for* 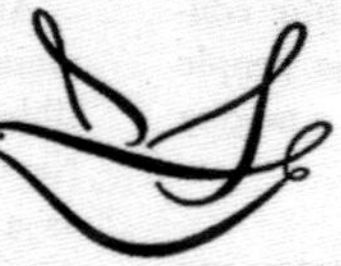 *freedom*

As we approach the third anniversary of the ruling of the United States Supreme Court against racially segregated public school systems, we invite all believers in the God-given concept of the brotherhood of man and in the American ideal of equality, to assemble, review the national scene, give thanks for the progress to date, and pray for the wiping out of the evils that still beset our nation.

The May 17, 1954, ruling against state-imposed segregation came about in orderly fashion, through the courts, from the lowest to the highest. Our appeal was based upon the Constitution of the United States of America. It was made after fifty-eight years of enduring the grossly unequal "separate-but-equal" doctrine laid down in 1896. It came after decades of patience and of reliance on morality and justice. It came slowly, step by step.

It came without violence, terror, or assassination. No bombs were thrown. No school shacks were burned down. No Jim Crow trains were dynamited. *What was then the law of the land was not defied.*

The Negro citizens of the land made the most of their circumstances. They got what education they could for their children. They "made out" with little or no public recreation. When they traveled they endured insult and physical assaults. They took such jobs as they could get at such wages as they were paid. They lived where they were herded. They were barred from the ballot boxes on election day. They abided by the kind of justice they received in the courts. They served their country in a Jim Crow army. They were victims of the bestial crime of lynching. However, this blanket of inequality and oppression did not completely smother the struggle for human rights. Time after time the challenge was met with steadfastness and courage, even in the face of disheartening odds. The valiant freedom fighters for civil rights became inspiring heroes for our time.

THE May 17 decision, then, was a New Emancipation. At last Negroes were to be recognized as citizens and the states were forbidden to set them off by law, solely because of race, in public education and elsewhere. In Montgomery the people caught the meaning of the hour and struck a mighty spiritual blow for human dignity.

On the public school question, nine states and the District of Columbia have either completed desegregation or have made a beginning. But eight states have defied the nation's highest court and have refused to begin in good faith, with all deliberate speed, to comply with its ruling. In these states privately organized groups have exerted economic pressure upon Negro citizens who have simply asked obedience to the Supreme Court. Men and women have been fired from their jobs. Merchants have been refused credit and goods. Farmers have been denied loans.

The governments of these states have joined the assault on democracy by moving to put the National Association for the Advancement of Colored People out of business. While the NAACP is the declared target of these actions, the true victims are the white and Negro citizens who are thereby restricted in the exercise of their right to freedom of speech, freedom of assembly and petition, and freedom to seek redress of grievances through the courts.

In view of the historic role the Association has played in the life of American Negroes, the attack upon it becomes a very special and particular one upon the constitutional rights of Negro citizens. Abridging the basic rights of citizens is in itself a high crime; but depriving them of the agency through which they have sought, in the courts, to secure these very rights is shameful compounding of the felony. It makes a mockery of citizenship.

The law enforcement agencies of these states have permitted violence to be visited upon individuals and institutions which oppose segregation. Ministers have been arrested, threatened and shot. Churches and homes have been bombed. School children have been threatened by mobs.

Accompanying all this has been a campaign of racial slander of the most vicious and reprehensible nature, typified by characterization of the Negro as inherently criminal and diseased, and as a mental incompetent.

THIS defiance, this legislative harassment, this economic pressure, this slander and violence have been encouraged by public officials, including Mayors, Governors, Attorneys General, and United States Senators.

At the Federal level the civil rights bill has been trimmed and delayed in the Congress by members from the states where defiance of the Supreme Court is state policy. The avowed purpose is either to whittle it down to nothing, or to kill it altogether.

One hundred years ago, in the Dred Scott decision, it was held that the Constitution did not include Negroes in its protection of the rights of citizens. Even though a war was fought and the Constitution amended, some states today are seeking to wipe out history and to restore to force the Dred Scott decision of 1857.

In the words of Abraham Lincoln, this is a nation "conceived in liberty and dedicated to the proposition that all men are created equal." We believe its people treasure the heritage of equality before the law. They uphold this principle because they know that every man, whatever his race, religion, or station, must be free if our nation is to remain strong.

WE believe Americans are deeply religious and wish to order their lives and their country according to the great moral truths to be found in our common religious heritage.

As the Founding Americans prayed for strength and wisdom in the wilderness of a new land, as the slaves and their descendants prayed for emancipation and human dignity, as men of every color and clime in time of crisis have sought Divine guidance, so we now, in these troubled and momentous years, call upon all who love justice and dignity and liberty, who love their country, and who love mankind, to join in a Prayer Pilgrimage to Washington on May 17, 1957, where we shall renew our strength, communicate our unity, and rededicate our efforts, firmly but peaceably, to the attainment of freedom.

A. Philip Randolph

A. PHILIP RANDOLPH
President, Brotherhood of Sleeping Car Porters, AFL-CIO

Martin L. King Jr.

REV. MARTIN LUTHER KING, JR.
President, Southern Leaders Conference

Roy Wilkins

ROY WILKINS
Executive Secretary National Association for the Advancement of Colored People

Washington, D.C.

April 5, 1957

"To arouse the conscience of the nation"

FOR INFORMATION WRITE TO:

Prayer Pilgrimage for Freedom

REV. THOMAS KILGORE, JR.	OR	REV. RALPH D. ABERNATHY
National Director		*Southern Director*
20 West 40th Street		First Baptist Church
New York 18, N. Y.		347 Ripley Street
		Montgomery, Alabama

ADDRESS BY REV. DR. MARTIN LUTHER KING, JR., PASTOR
THE DEXTER AVENUE BAPTIST CHURCH
PRESIDENT OF THE MONTGOMERY IMPROVEMENT ASSOCIATION
CHAIRMAN, THE SOUTHERN LEADERSHIP CONFERENCE
AT THE PRAYER PILGRIMAGE FOR FREEDOM AT
THE LINCOLN MEMORIAL, WASHINGTON, D. C.
MAY 17, 1957, 12:00 NOON.

Mr. Chairman, distinguished platform associates; fellow Americans. Three years ago the Supreme Court of this nation rendered in simple, eloquent and unequivocal language a decision which will long be stencilled on the mental sheets of succeeding generations. For all men of goodwill, this May 17th decision came as a joyous daybreak to end the long night of enforced segregation. It came as a great beacon light of hope to millions of disinherited people throughout the world who had dared only to dream of freedom. It came as a legal and sociological deathblow to the old Plessy Doctrine of "separate-but-equal." It came as a reaffirmation of the good old American doctrine of freedom and equality for all people.

Unfortunately, this noble and sublime decision has not gone without opposition. This opposition has often risen to ominous proportions. Many states have risen up in open defiance. The legislative halls of the south ring loud with such words as "interposition" and "nullification." Methods of defiance range from crippling economic reprisals to the tragic reign of violence and terror. All of these forces have conjoined to make for massive resistance.

But, even more, all types of conniving methods are still being used to prevent Negroes from becoming registered voters. The denial of this sacred right is a tragic betrayal of the highest mandates of our democratic tradition. So long as I do not firmly and irrevocably possess the right to vote I do not possess myself. I cannot make up my mind -- it is made up for me. I cannot live as a Democratic citizen, observing the laws I have helped to enact -- I can only submit to the edict of others. So our most urgent request to the President of the United States and every member of Congress is to give us the right to vote. Give us the ballot and we will no longer have to worry the Federal Government about our basic rights. Give us the ballot and we will no longer plead to the Federal Government for passage of an anti-lynching law; we will by the power of our vote write the law on the statute books of the southern states, and bring an end to the dastardly acts of the hooded perpetrators of violence. Give us the ballot and we will transform the salient misdeeds of blood thirsty mobs into the abiding good deeds of orderly citizens. Give us the ballot and we will fill our legislative halls with men of goodwill, and send to the sacred halls of Congress men who will not sign a southern manifesto because of their devotion to the manifesto of justice. Give us the ballot and we will place judges on the benches of the south who will "do justly and love mercy," and we will place at the head of the southern states governors who have felt not only the tang of the human, but the glow of the Divine. Give us the ballot and we will quietly and non-violently, without rancor or bitterness, implement the Supreme Court's Decision of May 17, 1954.

In this juncture of our nation's history there is an urgent need for dedicated and courageous leadership. If we are to solve the problems ahead and make racial justice a reality, this leadership must be fourfold.

First, there is need for strong, aggressive leadership from the Federal Government. So far, only the judicial branch of the government has evinced this quality of leadership. If the executive and legislative branches of the government were as concerned about the protection of our citizenship rights as the Federal Courts have been, then the transition from a segregated to an integrated society would be infinitely smoother. But we so often look to Washington in vain for this concern. In the midst of the tragic breakdown of law and order, the executive branch of the government is all too silent and apathetic. In the midst of the desperate need for civil rights legislation, the legislative branch of the government is all too stagnant and hypocritical.

This dearth of positive leadership from the Federal Government is not confined to one particular political party. Both parties have betrayed the cause of justice. The Democrats have betrayed it by capitulating to the prejudices and undemocratic practices of the southern Dixiecrats. The Republicans have betrayed it by capitulating to the blatant hypocrisy of right wing, reactionary northerners. These men so often have a high blood pressure of words and an anemia of deeds.

In the midst of these prevailing conditions, we come to Washington today pleading with the President and the members of Congress to provide a strong, moral and courageous leadership for a situation that cannot permanently be evaded. We come humbly to say to the men in the forefront of our government that the Civil Rights issue is not an ephemeral, evanescent domestic issue that can be kicked about by reactionary guardians of the status quo; it is rather an eternal moral issue which may well determine the destiny of our nation in the ideological struggle with Communism. The hour is late. The clock of destiny is ticking out. We must act now, before it is too late.

A second area in which there is need for strong leadership is from white northern liberals. There is a dire need today for a liberalism which is truly liberal. What we are witnessing today in so many northern communities is a sort of quasi-liberalism which is based on the principle of looking sympathetically at all sides. It is a liberalism so bent on seeing all sides, that it fails to become committed to either side. It is a liberalism that is so objectively analytical that it is not subjectively commited. It is a liberalism which is neither hot nor cold, but lukewarm. We call for a liberalism from the north which will be thoroughly committed to the ideal of racial justice and will not be deterred by the propaganda and subtle words of those who say, "slow up for a while, you are pushing too fast."

A third source that we must look to for strong leadership is from the moderates of the white south. It is unfortunate, indeed, that at this time the leadership of the white south stems from the close-minded reactionaries. These persons gain prominence and power by the dissemination of false ideas, and by deliberately appealing to the deepest hate responses within the human mind.

It is my firm belief that this close-minded, reactionary, recalcitrant group constitutes a numerical minority. There are in the white south more open-minded moderates than appears on the surface. These persons are silent today because of fear of social, political and economic reprisals. God grant that the white moderates of the south will rise up courageously, without fear, and take up the leadership in this tense period of transition.

I cannot close without stressing the urgent need for strong, courageous and intelligent leadership from the Negro community. We need a leadership that is calm and yet positive. This is no day for the rabble-rouser, whether he be Negro or white. We must realize that we are grappling with the most weighty social problem of this nation, and in grappling with such a complex problem there is no place for misguided emotionalism. We must work passionately and unrelentingly for the goal of freedom, but we must be sure that our hands are clean in the struggle. We must never struggle with falsehood, hate or malice. We must never become bitter. I know how we feel sometime. There is the danger that those of us who have been forced so long to stand amid the tragic midnight of oppression, those of us who have been trampled over, those of us who have been kicked about, will become bitter. But if we will become bitter and indulge in hate campaigns the new order which is emerging will be nothing but a duplication of the old order.

We must meet hate with love. We must meet physical force with soul force. There is still a voice crying out through the vistas of time, saying: "Love your enemies, bless them that curse you, pray for them that despitefully use you. Then, and only then, can you matriculate into the university of eternal life." That same voice cries out in terms lifted to cosmic proportions: "He who lives by the sword will perish by the sword." History is replete with the bleached bones of nations that failed to follow this command. We must follow non-violence and love.

Now, I am not talking about a sentimental, affectionate kind of love, I am not talking about <u>eros</u>, which is a sort of aesthetic, romantic love. I am not even talking about <u>philia</u> which is a sort of intimate affectionateness between personal friends. I am talking about <u>agape</u> -- I'm talking about the love of God working in the hearts of men. I am talking about the type of love that will cause you to love the person who does the evil deed, while hating the deed that the person does. We must love.

There is another warning signal. We talk a great deal about our rights, and rightly so. We proudly proclaim that three-fourths of the peoples of the world are colored. We have the privilege of noticing in our generation the great drama of freedom and independence as it unfolds in Asia and Africa. All of these things are in line with the unfolding work of Providence. We must be sure, however, that we accept them in the right spirit. We must not seek to use our emerging freedom and our growing power to do the same thing to the white minority that has been done to us for so many centuries. Our aim must never be to defeat or humiliate the white man. We must not become victimized with a philosophy of black supremacy. God is not interested in merely freeing black men and brown men and yellow men; God is interested in freeing the whole human race. We must work with determination to create a society in which all men will live together as brothers and respect the dignity and worth of human personality.

We must also avoid the temptation of being victimized with a psychology of victors. We have won marvelous victories through the work of the NAACP. We have been able to do some of the most amazing things of this generation, and I come this afternoon with nothing but praise for this great organization. Although they outlaw the NAACP in Alabama and other states, the fact still remains that this organization has done more to achieve civil rights for Negroes than any other organization we can point to. Certainly this is marvelous. We must not, however, remain satisfied with a court victory over our white brothers. We must respond to every decision with an understanding of those who have opposed us, and with an acceptance of the new adjustments that the court orders pose for them. We must act in such a way as to make possible a coming together of white people on the basis of a real harmony of interest and understanding. We must seek an integration based on mutual respect.

I conclude by saying that each of us must keep faith in the future. Let us not despair. Let us realize that as we struggle for justice and freedom we have cosmic companionship. This is the long faith of the Hebraic-Christian tradition. The God that we worship is not some Aristotelian, "unmoved, mover" who merely contemplates upon himself; He is not merely a self-knowing God, but an other loving God who forever works through history for the establishment of His kingdom.

Those of us who call the name of Jesus Christ find something of an event in our Christian faith which tells us this. There is something in our faith that says to us, never despair, never give up, never feel that the cause of righteousness and justice is doomed. There is something in our Christian faith, at the center of it, which says to us that Good Friday may occupy the throne for a day, but ultimately it must give way to the triumphant beat of the drums of Easter. There is something in our faith which says that evil may so shape events that Caesar will occupy a palace and Christ a Cross, but one day that same Christ will rise up and split history into A.D. and B.C., so that even the life of Caesar must be dated by His name. There is something in this universe which justifies Carlyle in saying: "No lie can live forever." There is something in this universe which justifies William Cullen Bryant in saying: "Truth crushed to earth will rise again." There is something in this universe which justifies James Russell Lowell in saying: "Truth forever on the scaffold, wrong forever on the throne. Yet that scaffold sways the future, and behind the dim unknown stands God -- within the shadow, keeping watch above His own." Go out with that faith today; go back to your homes in the southland with that faith today; go back to Philadelphia, to New York, to Detroit and Chicago with that faith today. The universe is on our side in the struggle. Stand up for justice. Sometimes it gets hard; it is always difficult to get out of Egypt, the Red Sea always stands before you with discouraging dimensions. Even after you have crossed the Red Sea, you have to move through a wilderness with prodigious hilltops of evil, and gigantic mountains of opposition. But I say to you this afternoon: Keep moving. Let nothing slow you up. Move on with dignity, love and respectability.

I realize that it will occasionally cause restless nights. It might result in losing a job; it will cause suffering and sacrifice. It might even cause physical death for some. But if physical death is the price that some must pay to free their children from a permanent life of psychological death, then nothing can be more Christian. Keep moving amid every obstacle; keep moving amid every mounting of opposition. If you will do this with dignity -- when the history books are written in future years the historians will have to look back and say, there lived a great people, a people with "fleecy locks and black complexion" who injected a new dimension of love into the veins of civilization, a people who stood up with dignity and honor and saved Western civilization in her darkest hour. When that happens, "the morning stars will sing together, and the sons of God will shout for joy."

YALE UNIVERSITY ART GALLERY

Lee Friedlander's master set of photographs documenting the
1957 Prayer Pilgrimage for Freedom march has been gifted by the artist
to the Yale University Art Gallery, in New Haven, Connecticut.
In 2017, the photographs will be publicly exhibited for the first time,
in commemoration of the sixtieth anniversary of this historic event
in the American Civil Rights Movement.
The exhibition is curated by La Tanya Autry, the Marcia Brady Tucker Fellow,
Department of Modern and Contemporary Art, Yale University Art Gallery.
After its presentation at the Gallery,
the exhibition will travel to additional U.S. venues.

ACKNOWLEDGMENTS

Our deep gratitude goes to the following individuals and organizations without whose contributions this publication would not have been possible.

Heather Althoff and Donald Bailey, The Statesman Foundation; Charles C. Bergman; Akeel Bilgrami; Dorothy Blackmun; Sandra Butler; Melody Cleven and Mike Lynch; Joan Davidson and Ann Birckmayer, Furthermore; Adam Farron and Michael Feit; Fraenkel Gallery; Maria Friedlander; Allen Greenberg; Stephen Hilger; Andrew Hughes; Arlette and Gus Kayafas; Constance and Pete Kayafas; Albert Kresch; Nancy Lassalle; Cynthia Lewis, The King Center; Bill Mindlin; Kahlil Gibran Muhammad; Elizabeth O'Brien; Thomas Osborne; Pace/MacGill Gallery; Martin Peretz; Darryl Pinckney; Jock Reynolds and Tiffany Sprague, Yale University Art Gallery; Toni and Anthony Riocci; Mildred Roxborough, National Association for the Advancement of Colored People; Laura Starrett; Isabelle and James Storey; Nancy Sullivan; Philip Susswein; David and Candace Weir Foundation

Research: Heather Althoff and Karen Lee

Lee Friedlander Archivist: Stephanie Prussin

Design and typography in Century and Clarendon types by Katy Homans

Duotone separations by Thomas Palmer

Printed by Meridian Printing, East Greenwich, Rhode Island

under the supervision of Daniel Frank

Bound by Riverside Bindery, Rochester, New York